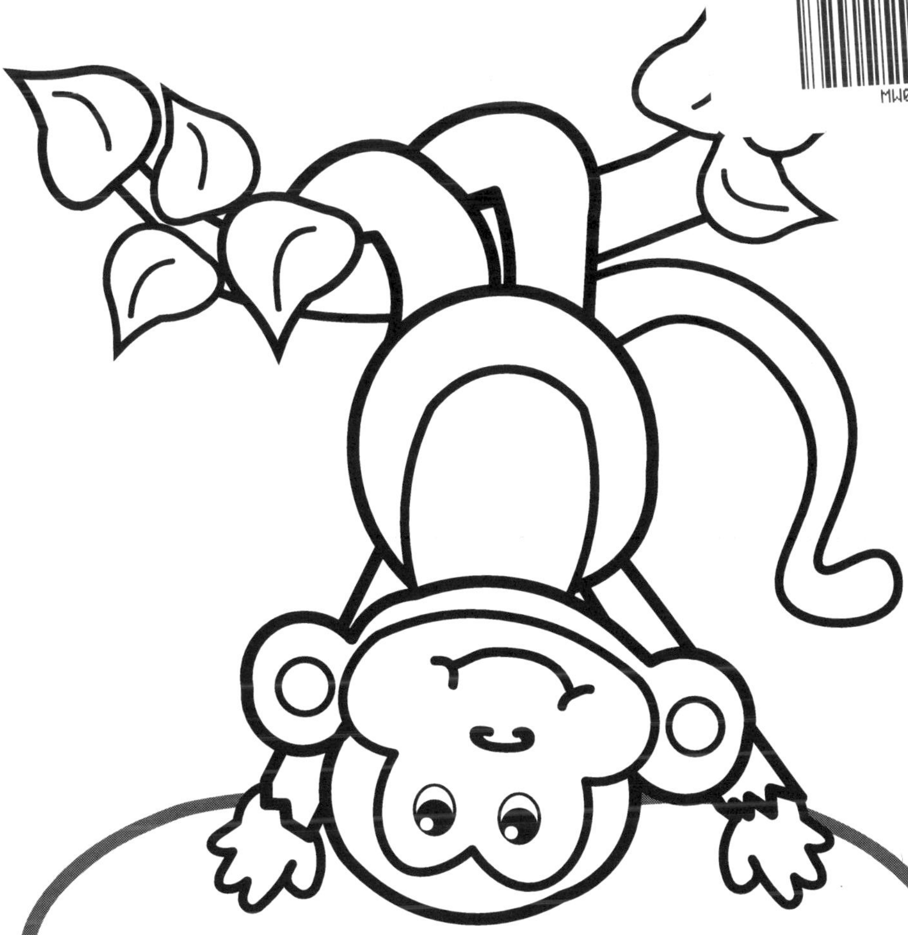

This Book Belongs to...

____

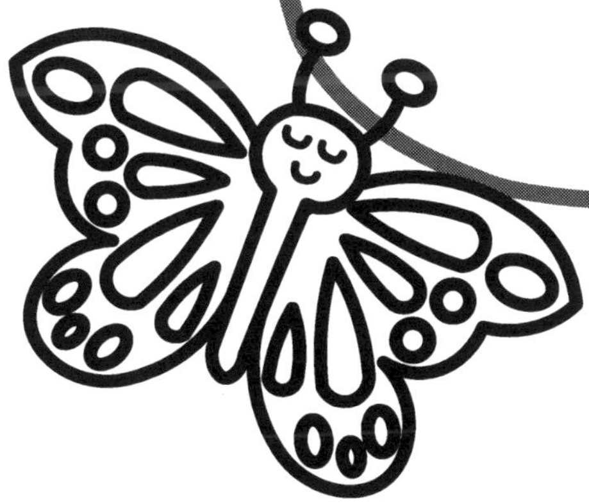

NYX
Spectrum

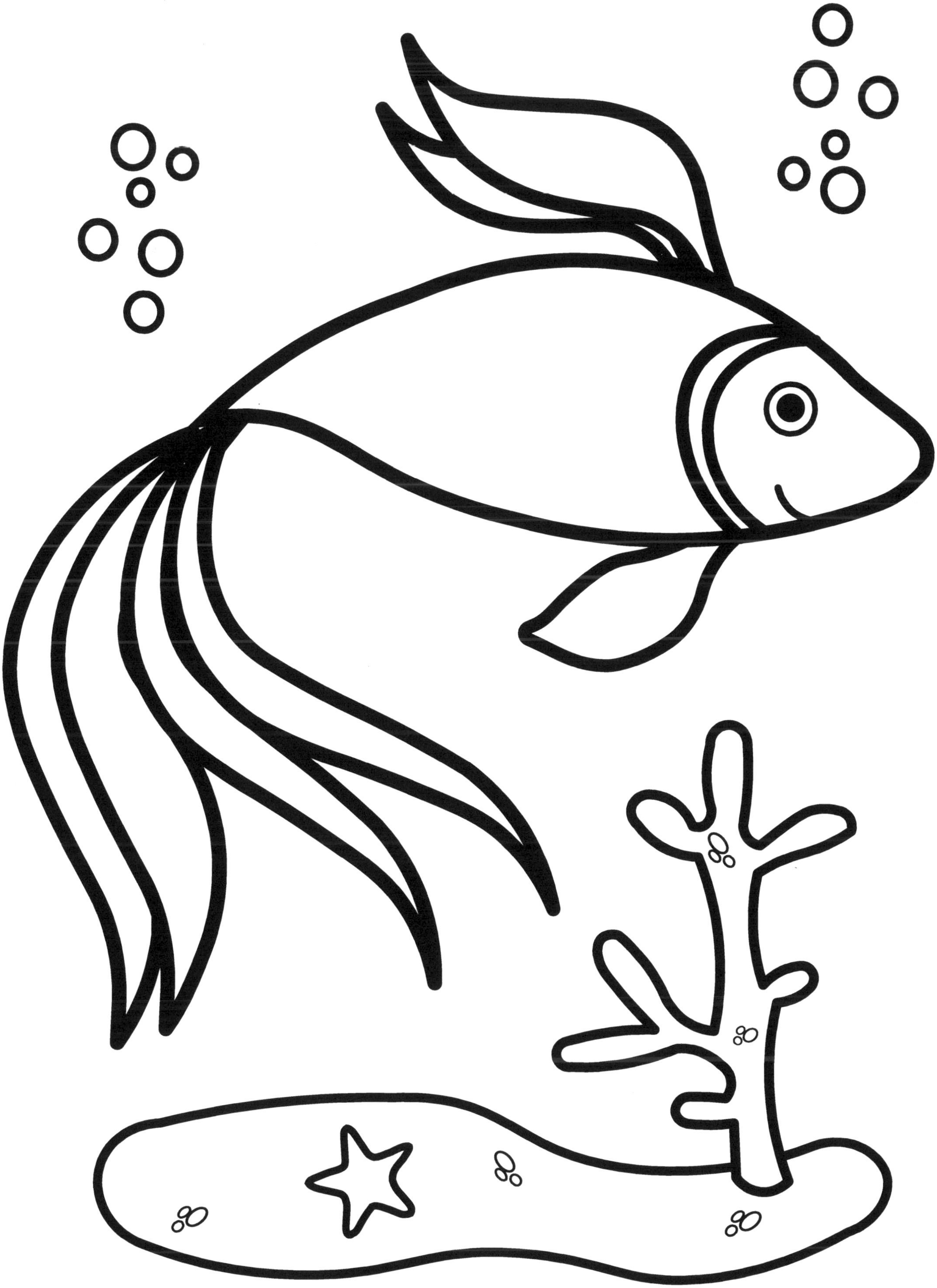

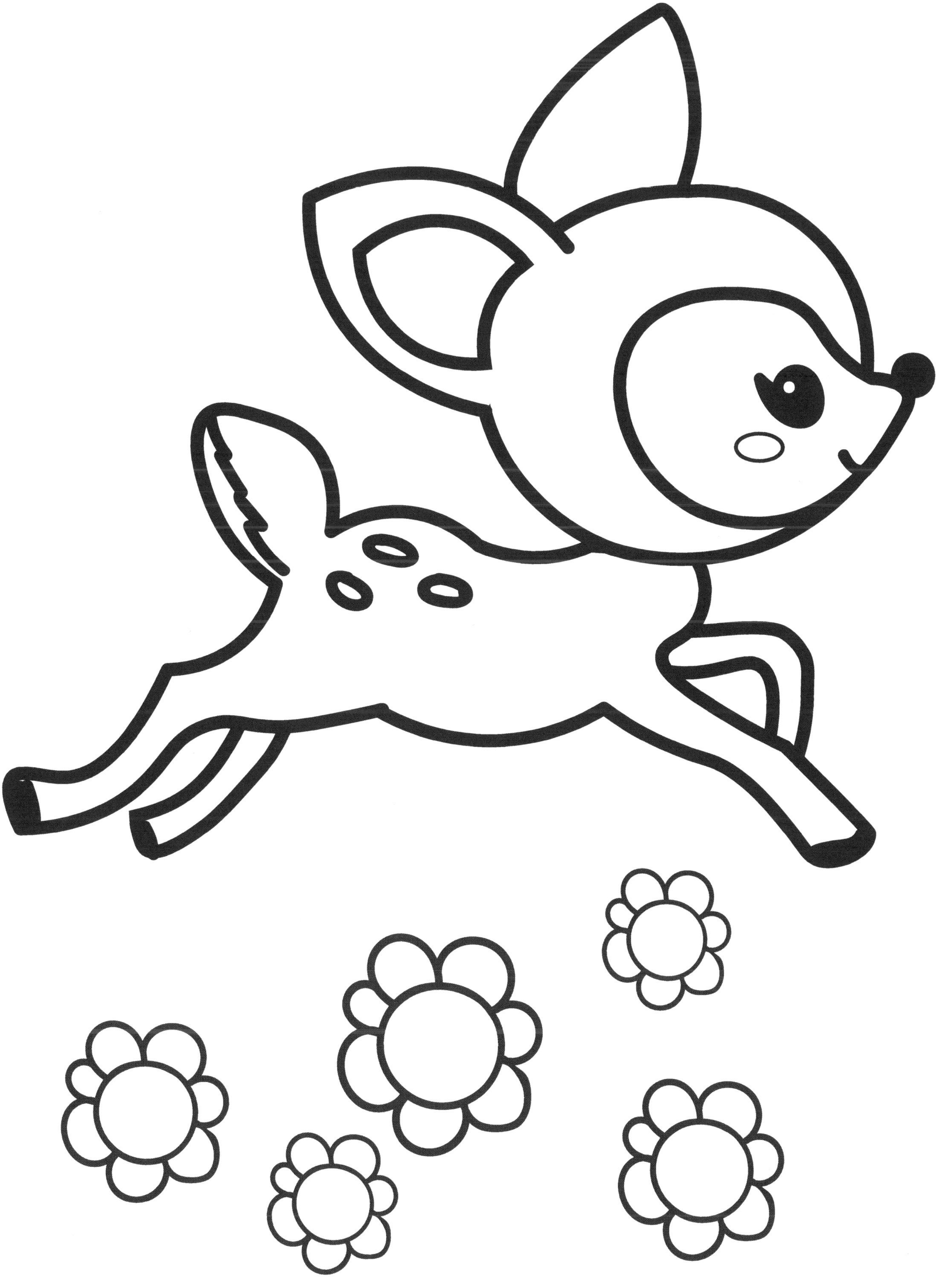

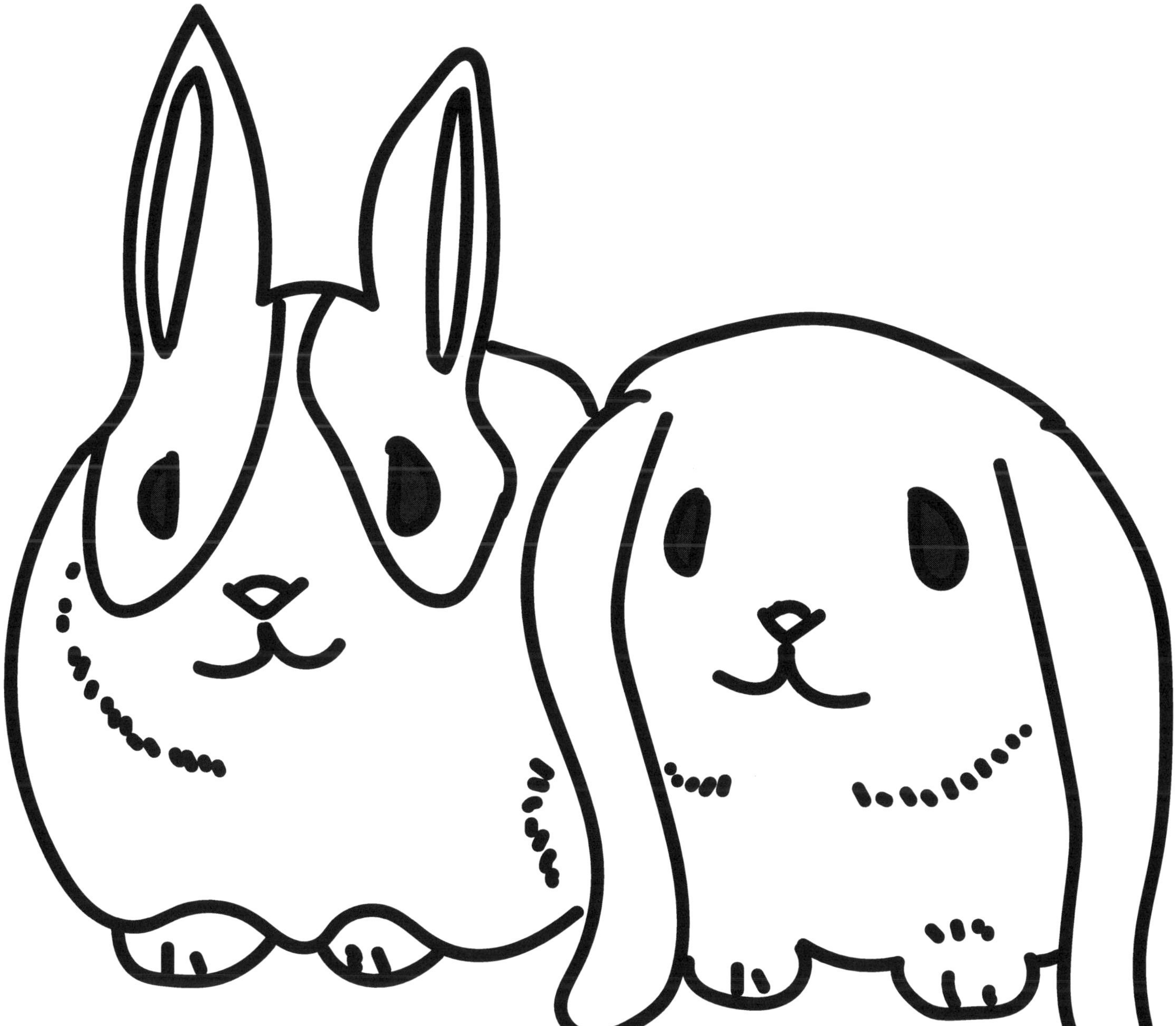

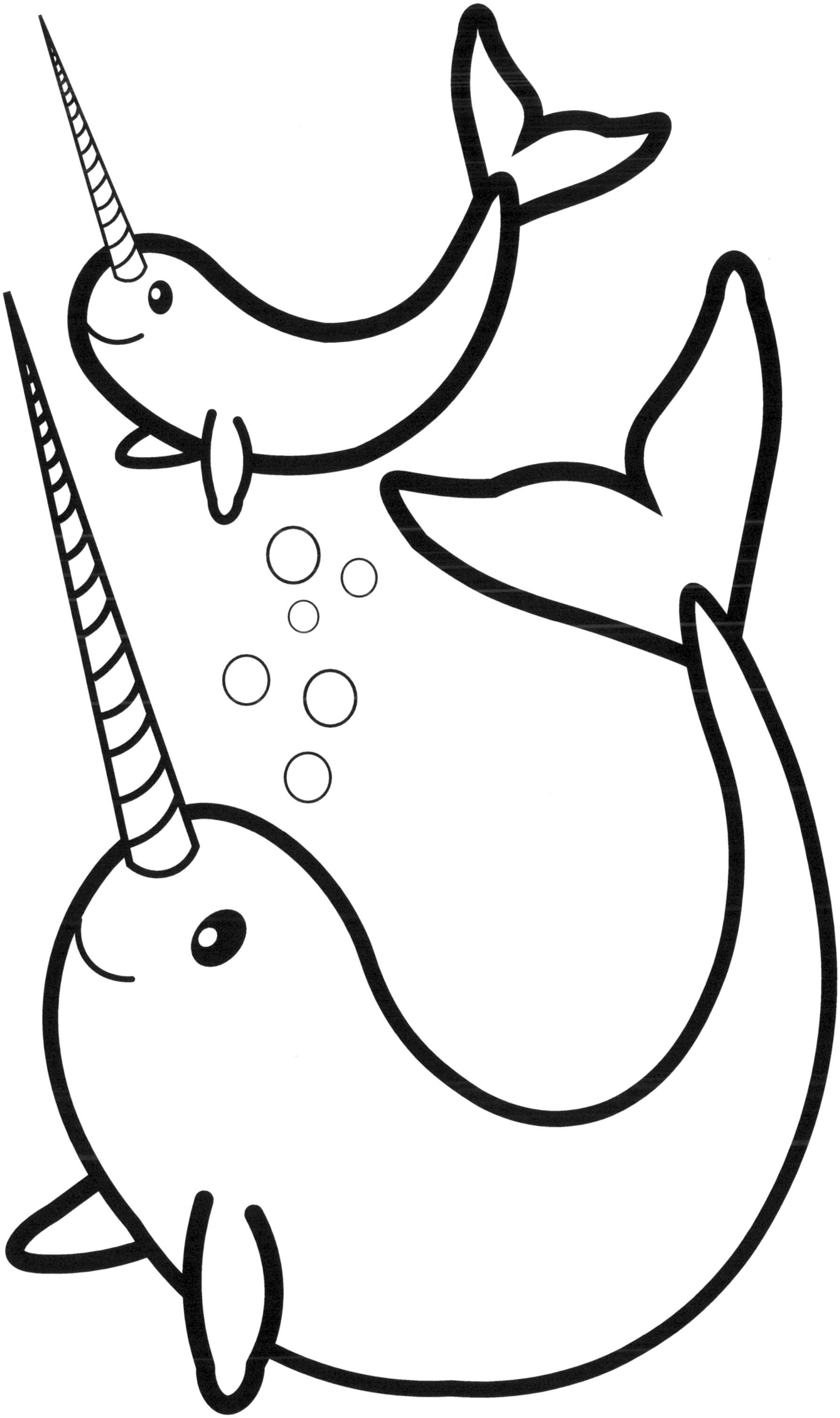

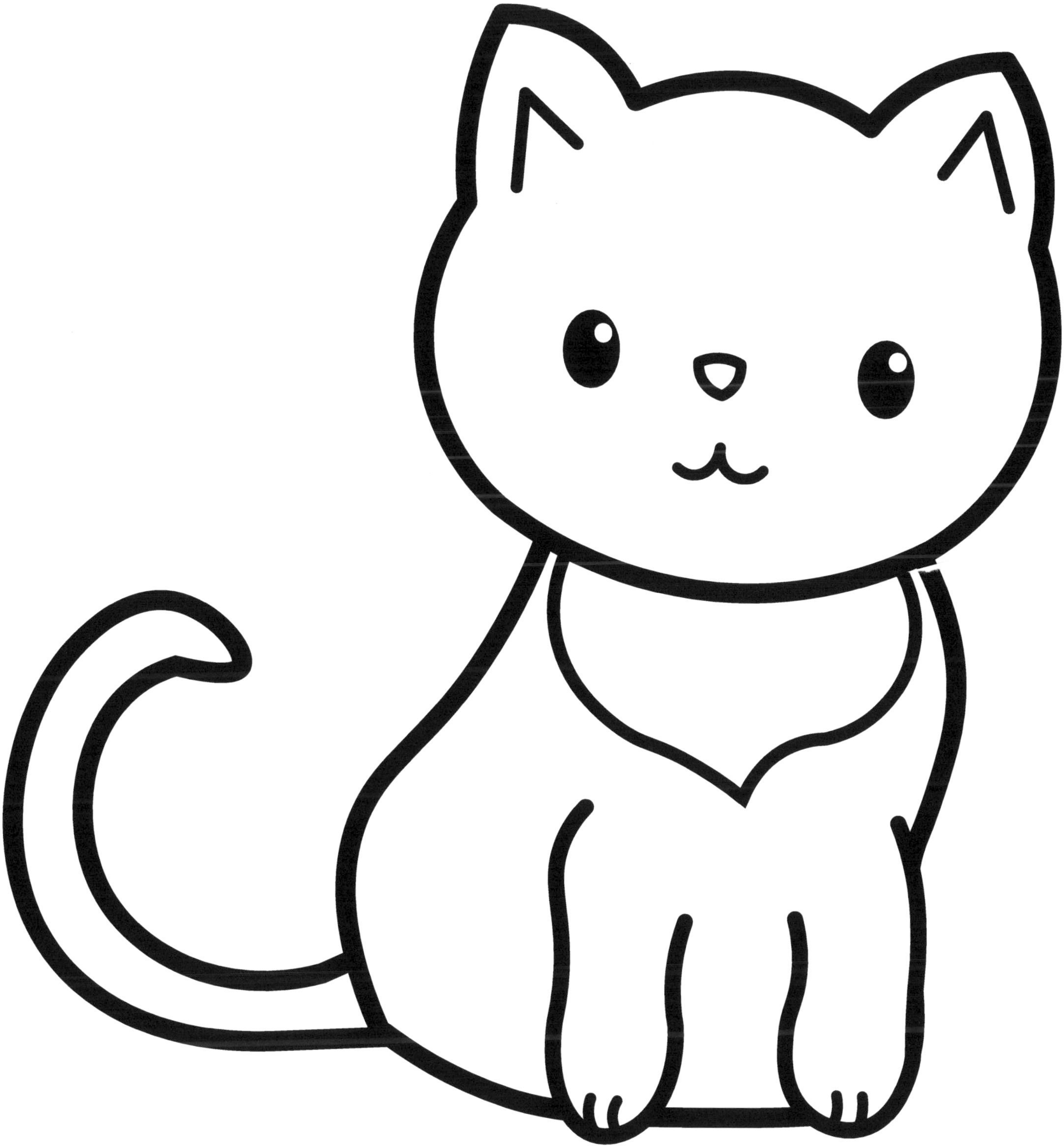

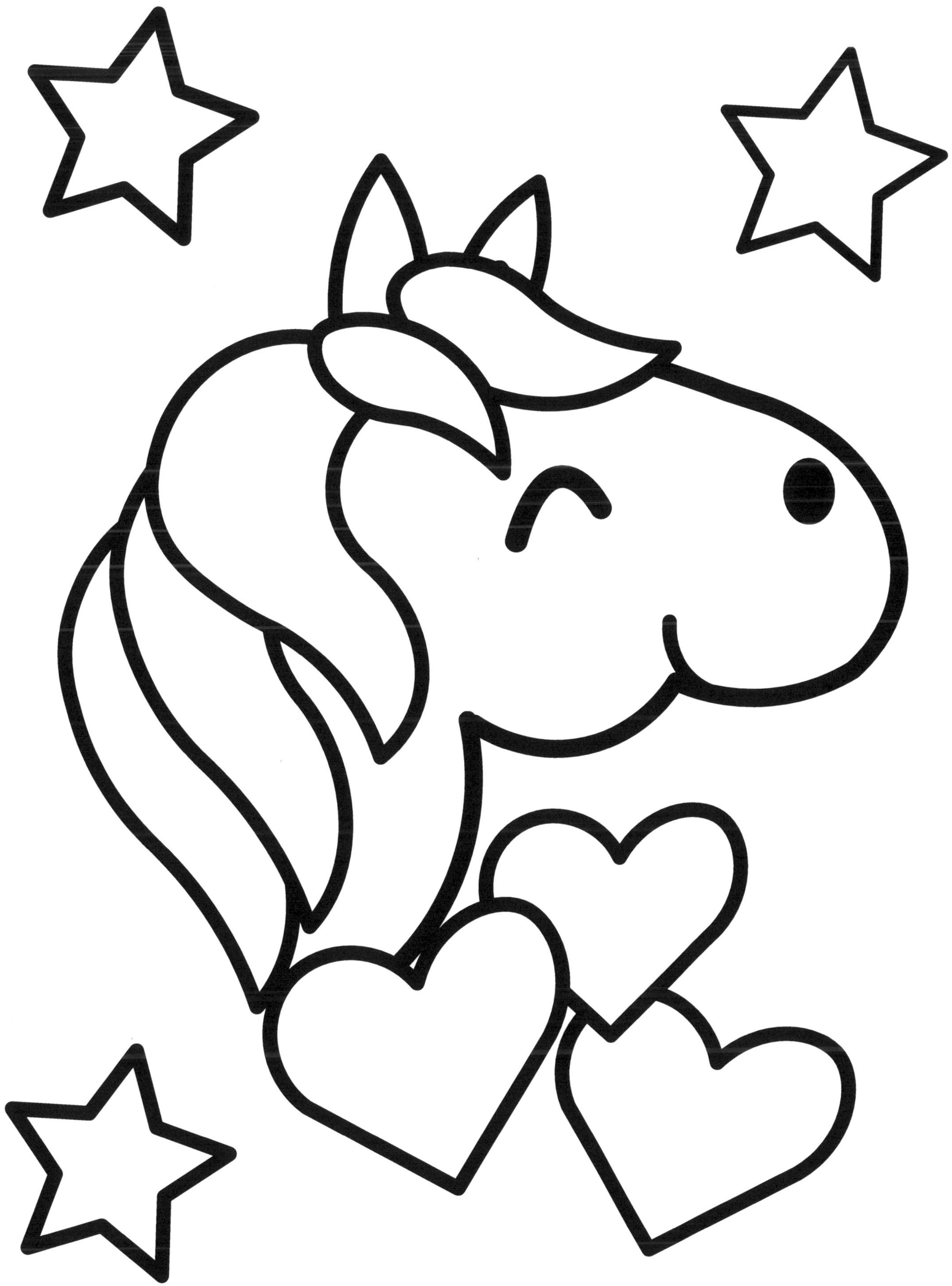

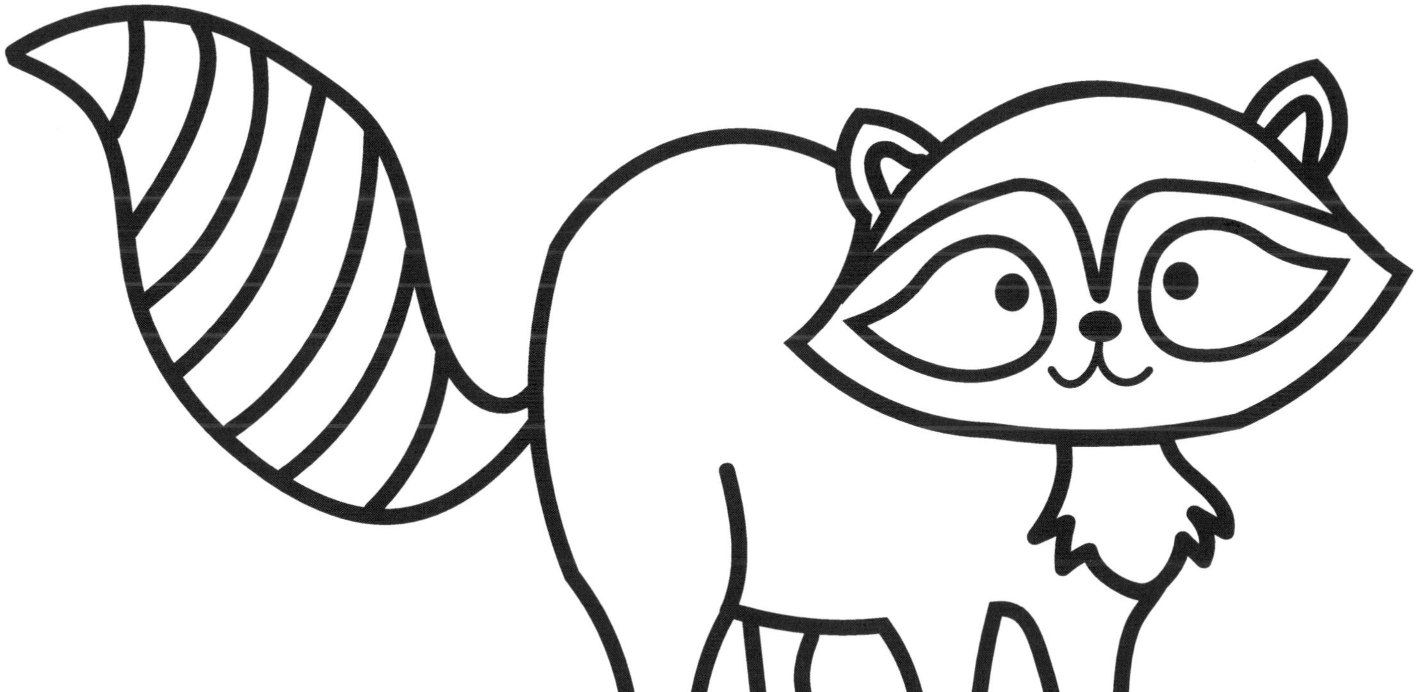

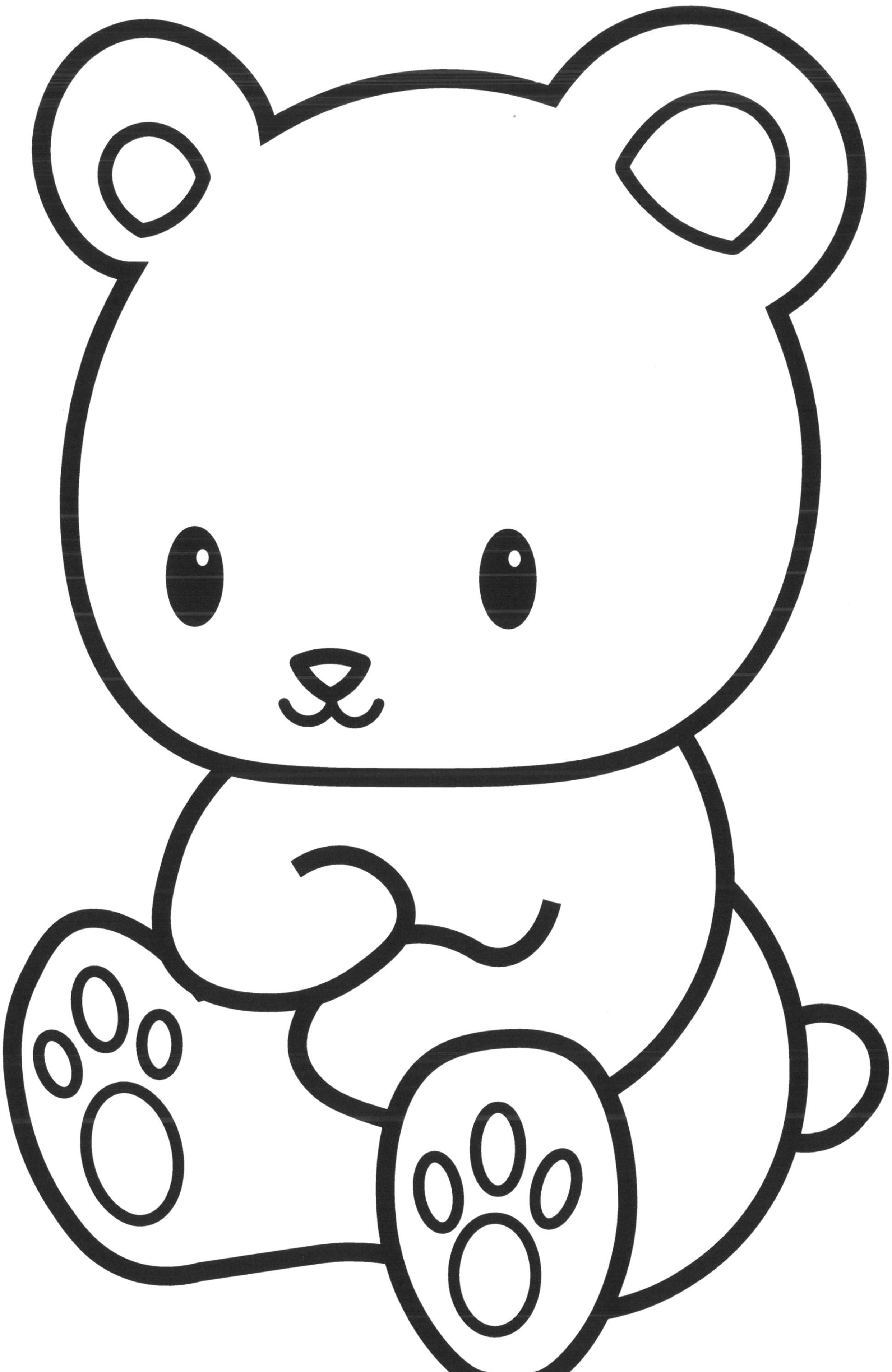

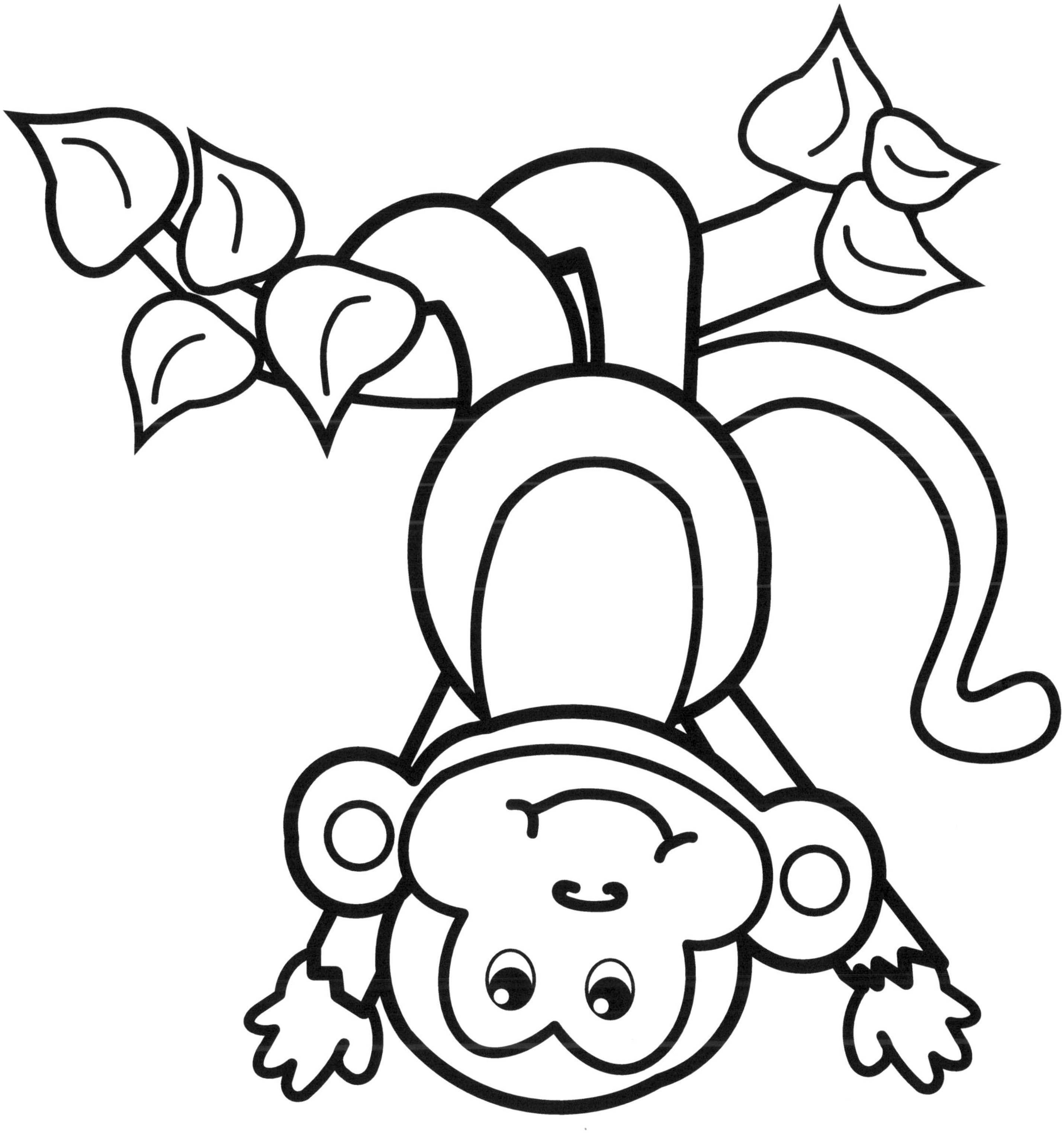

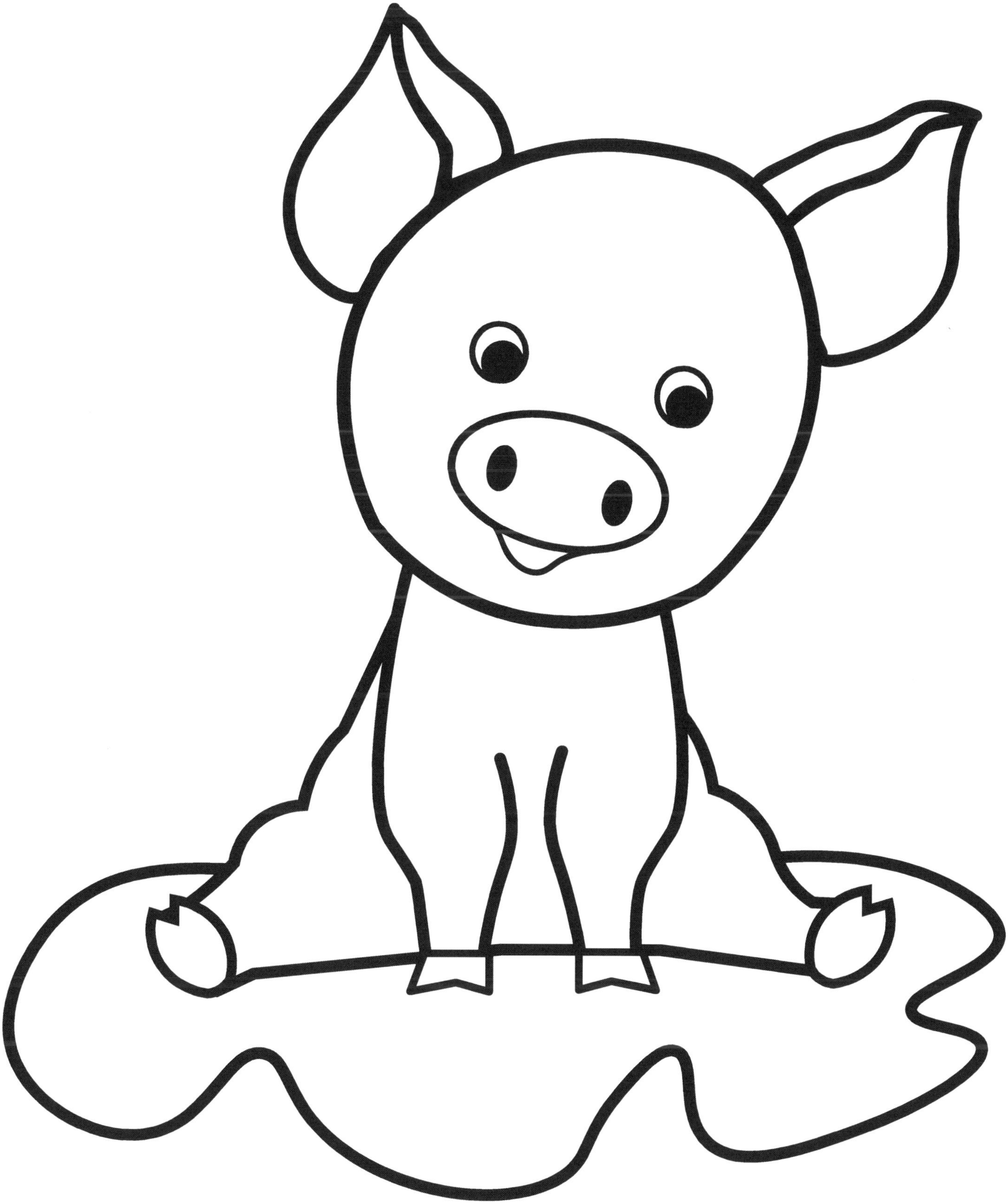

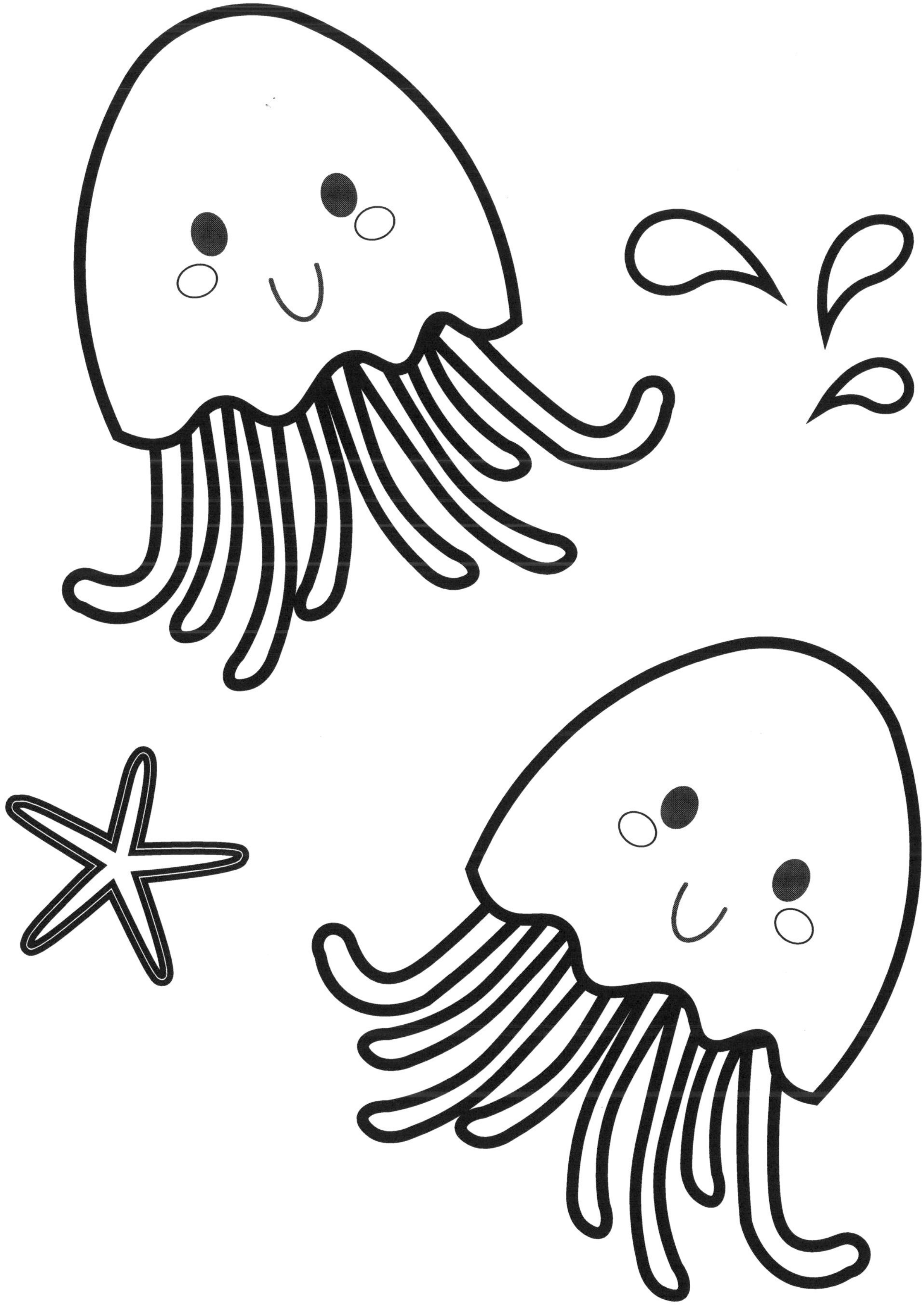

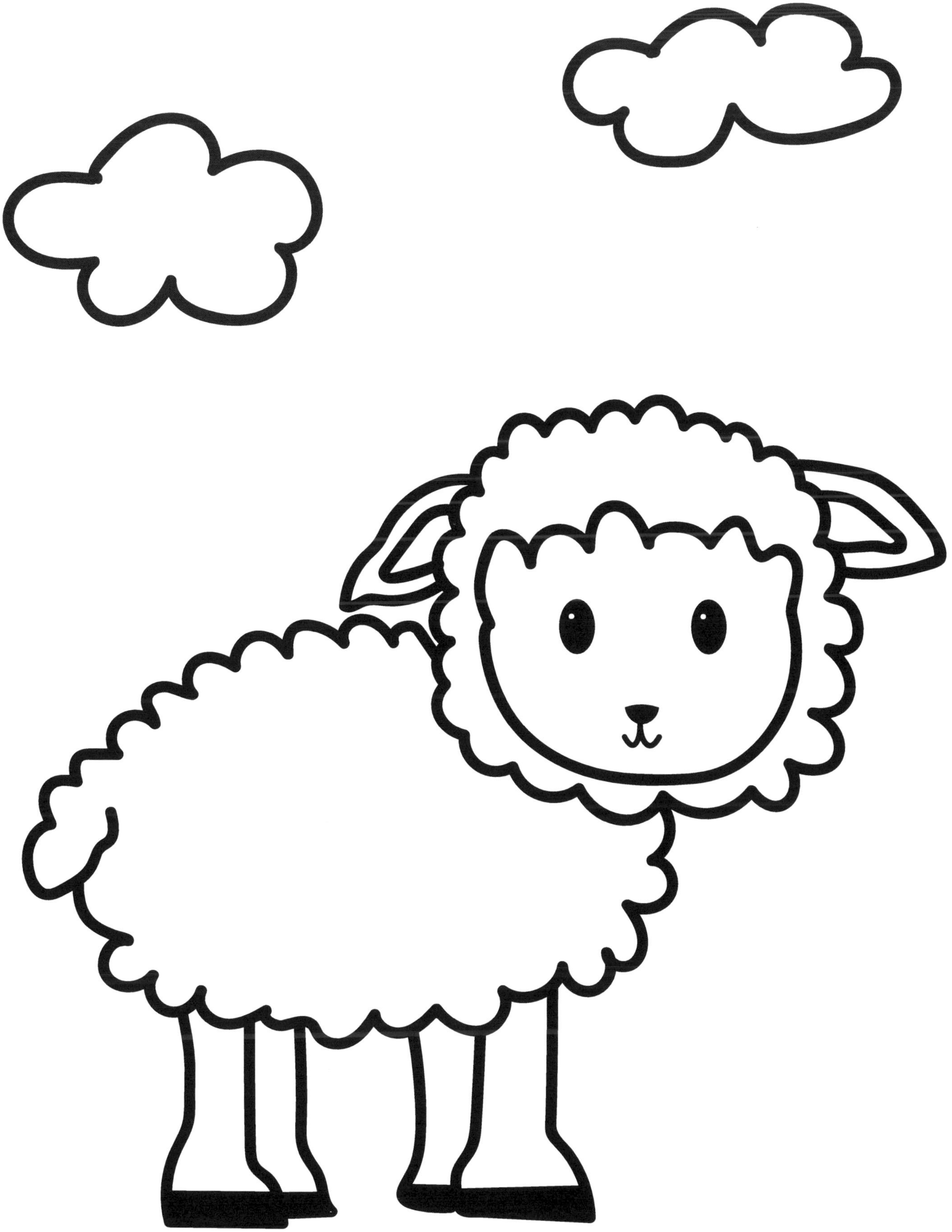

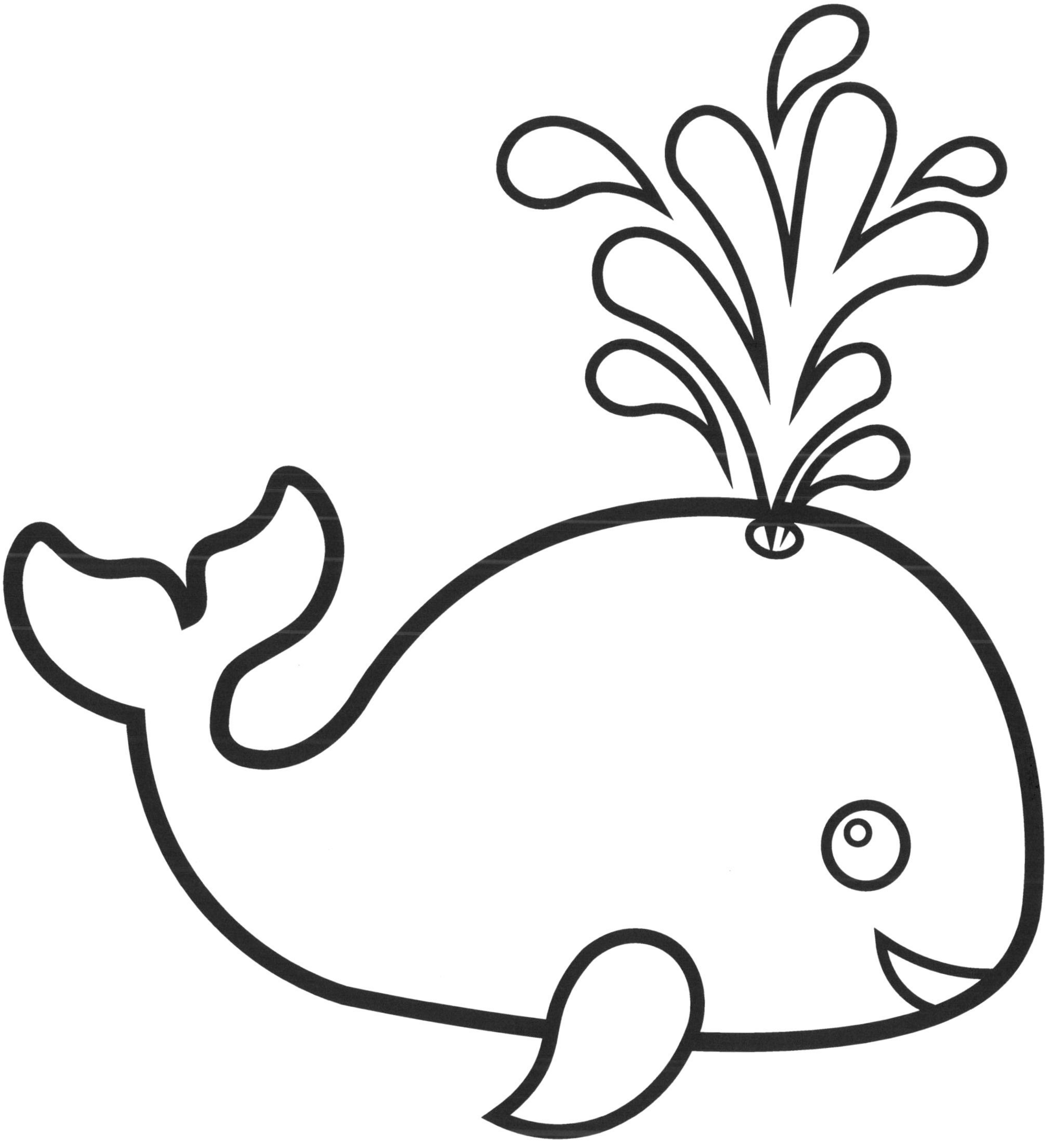

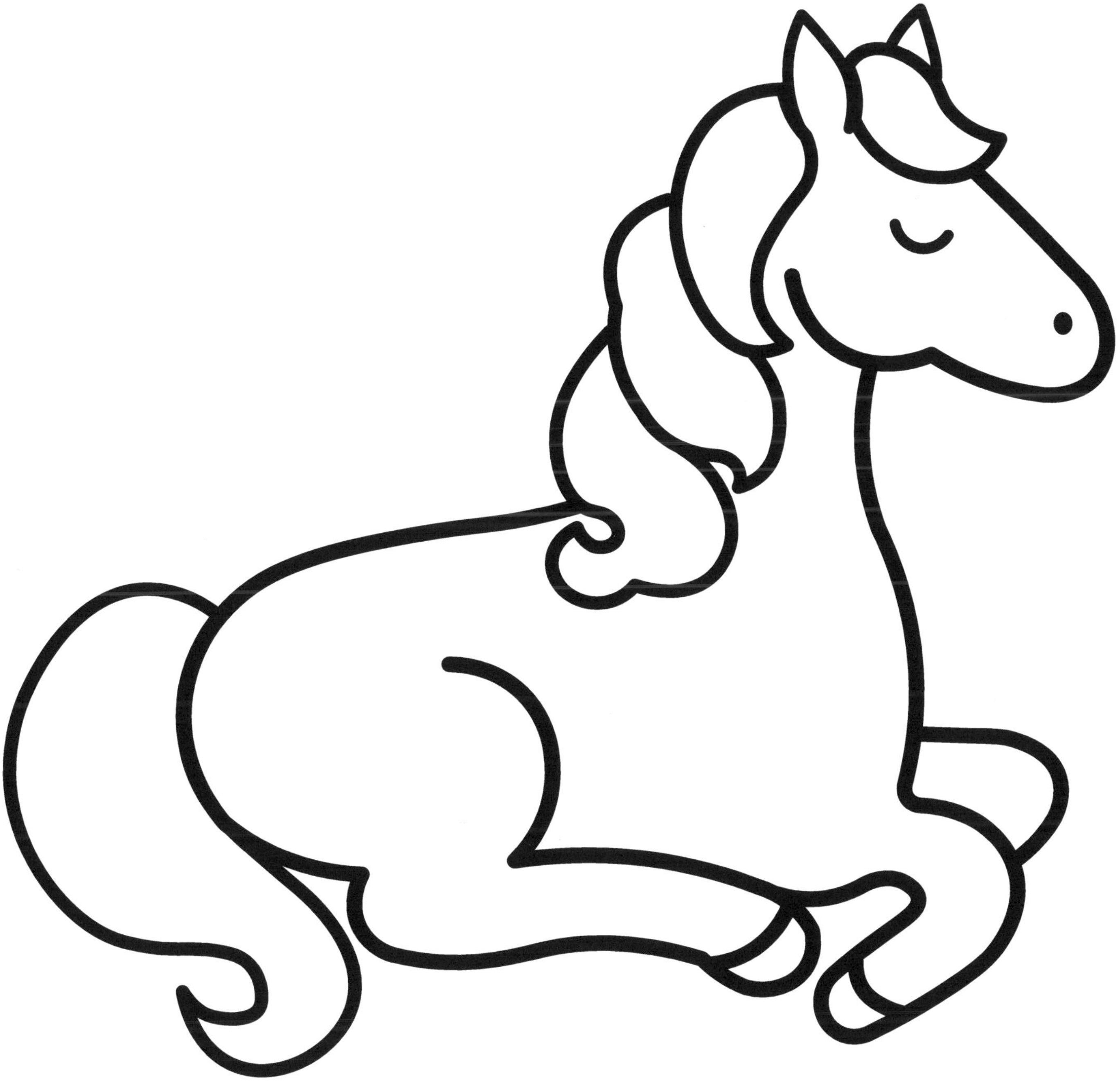

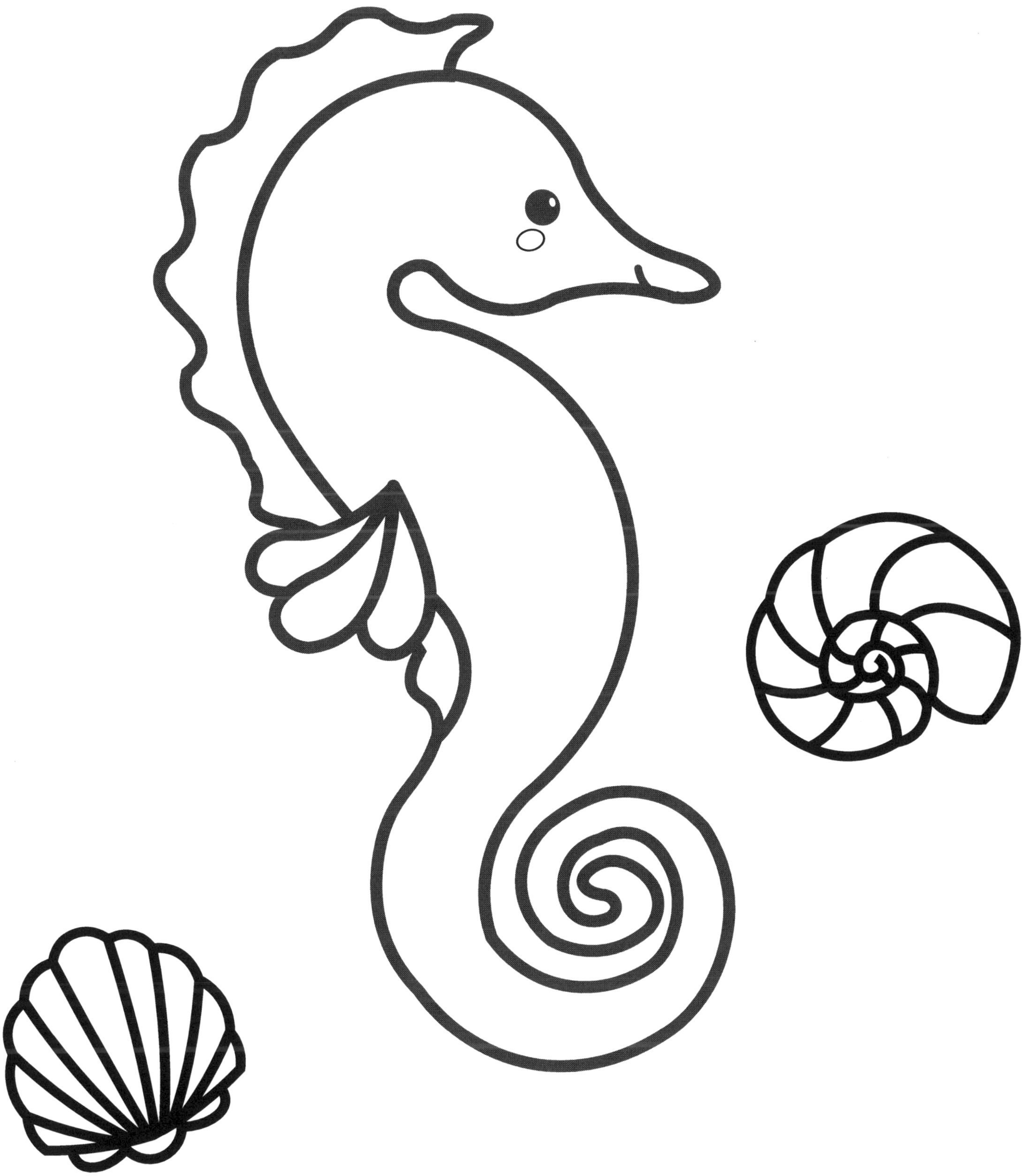

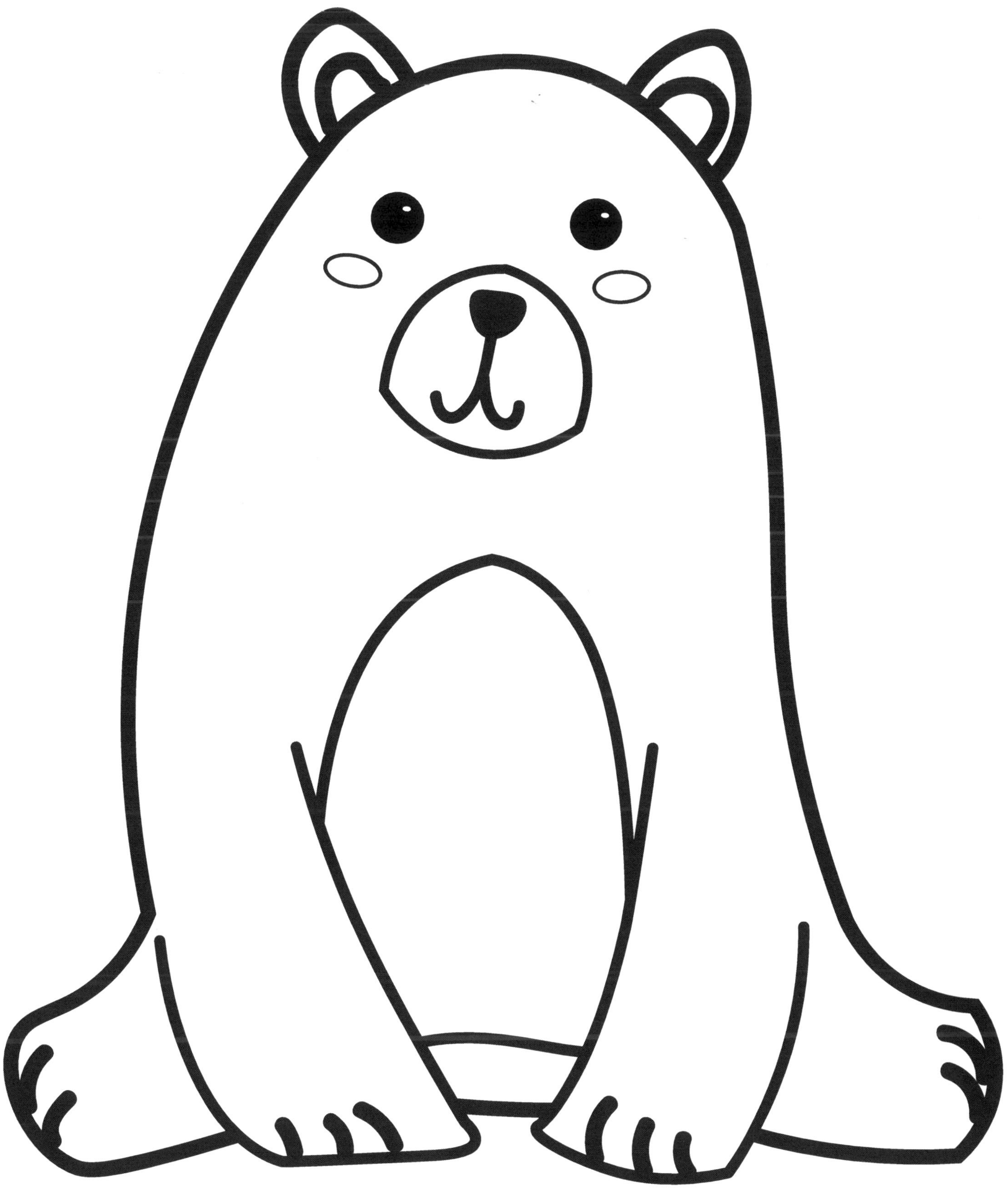

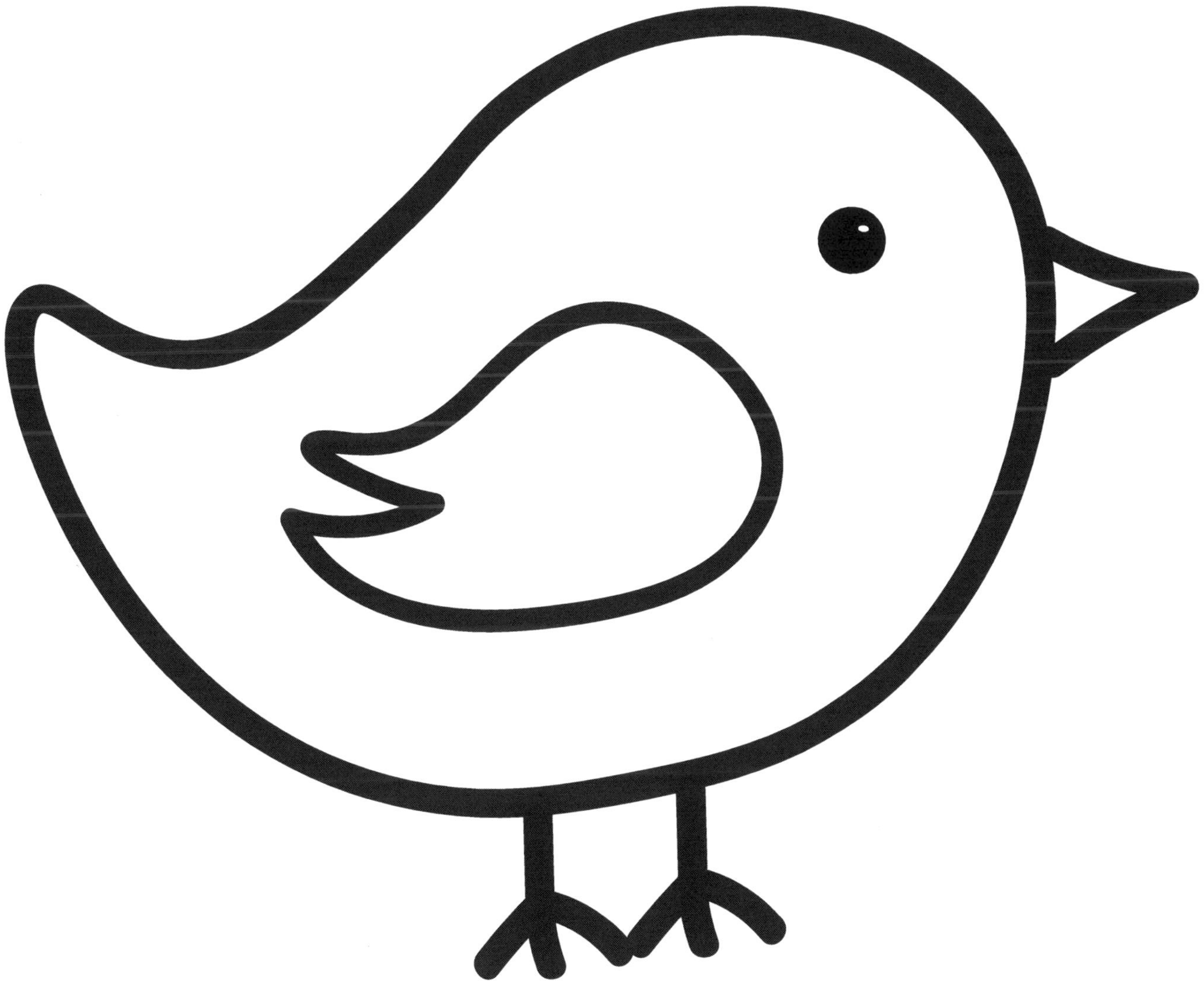

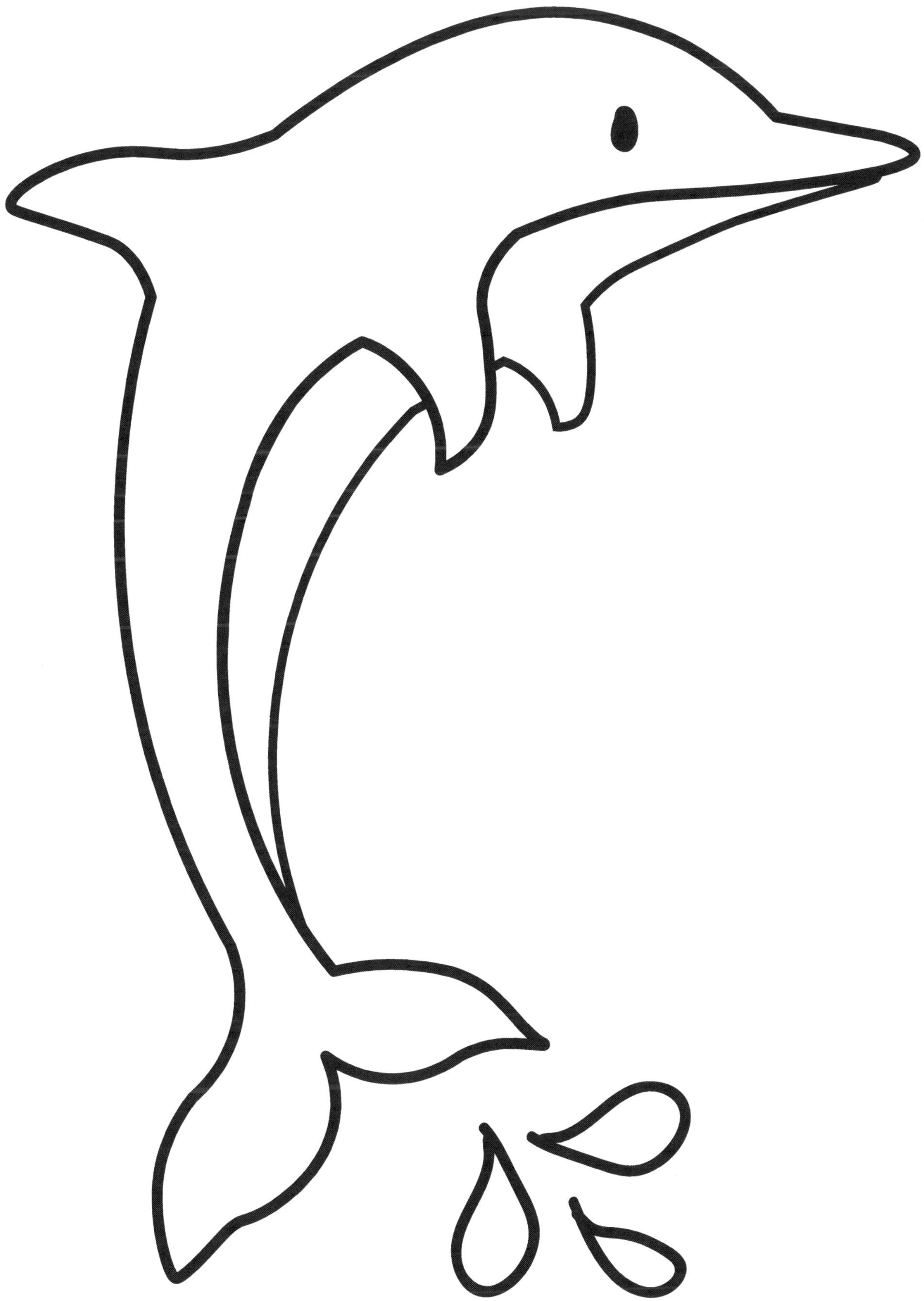

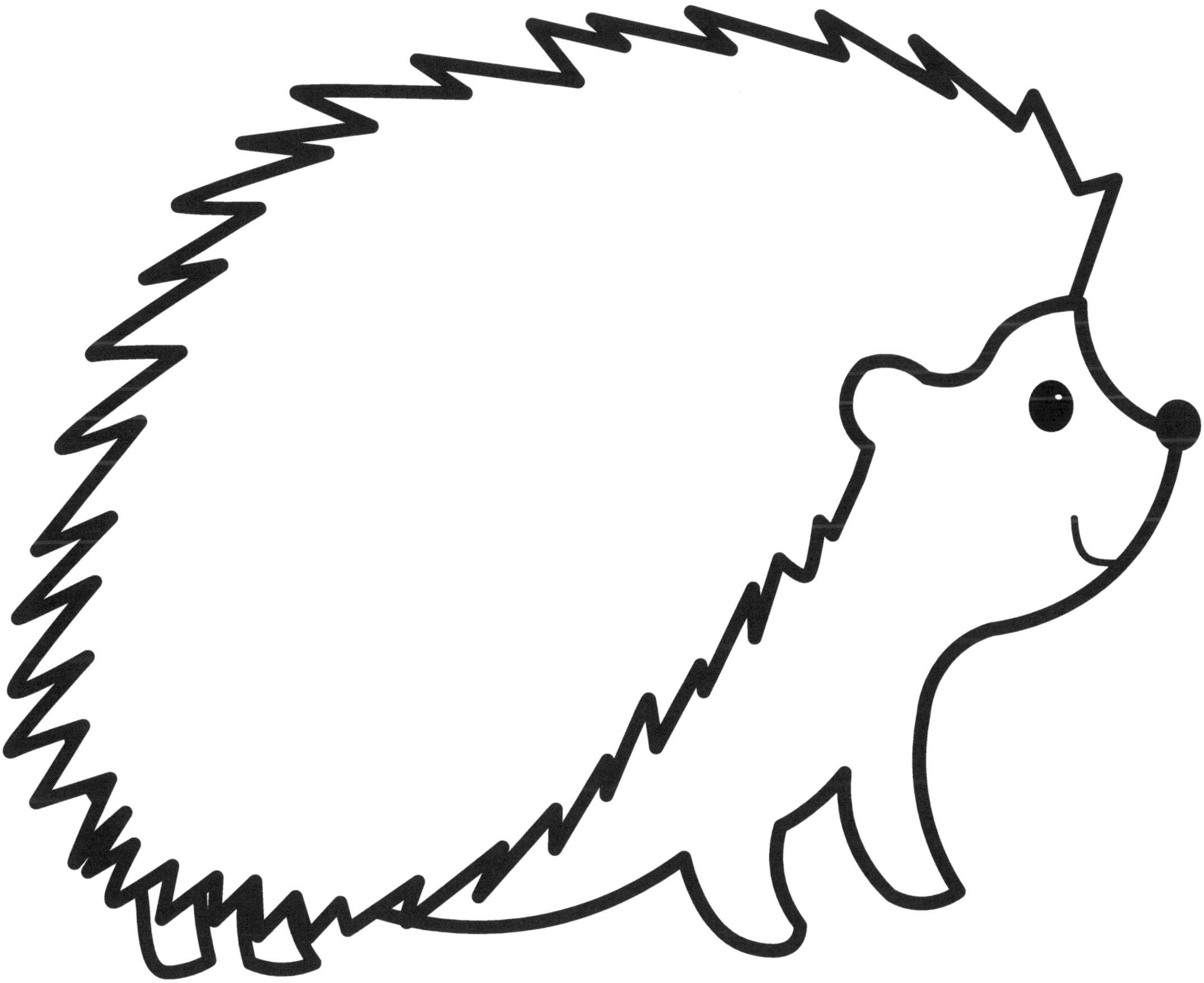

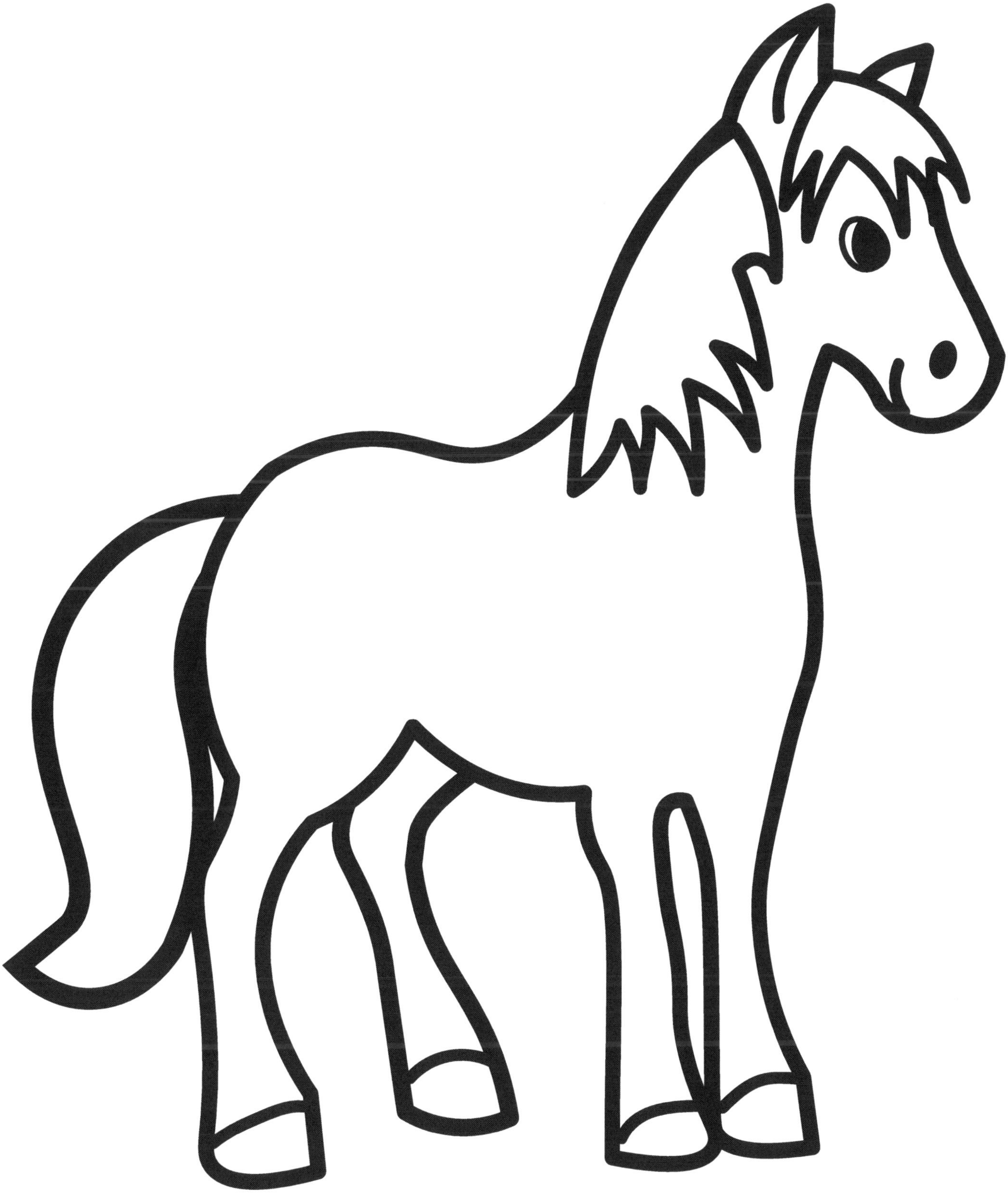

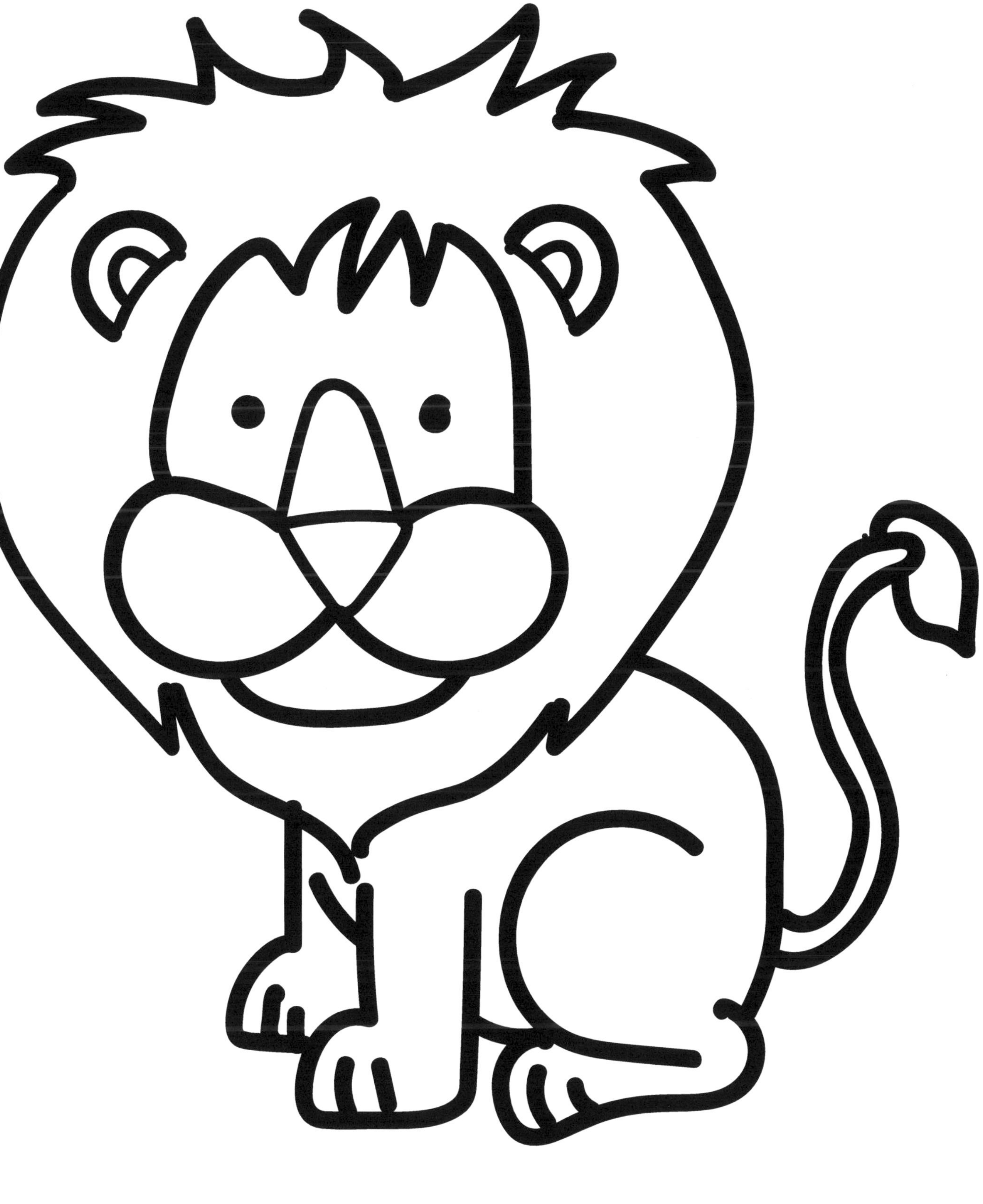

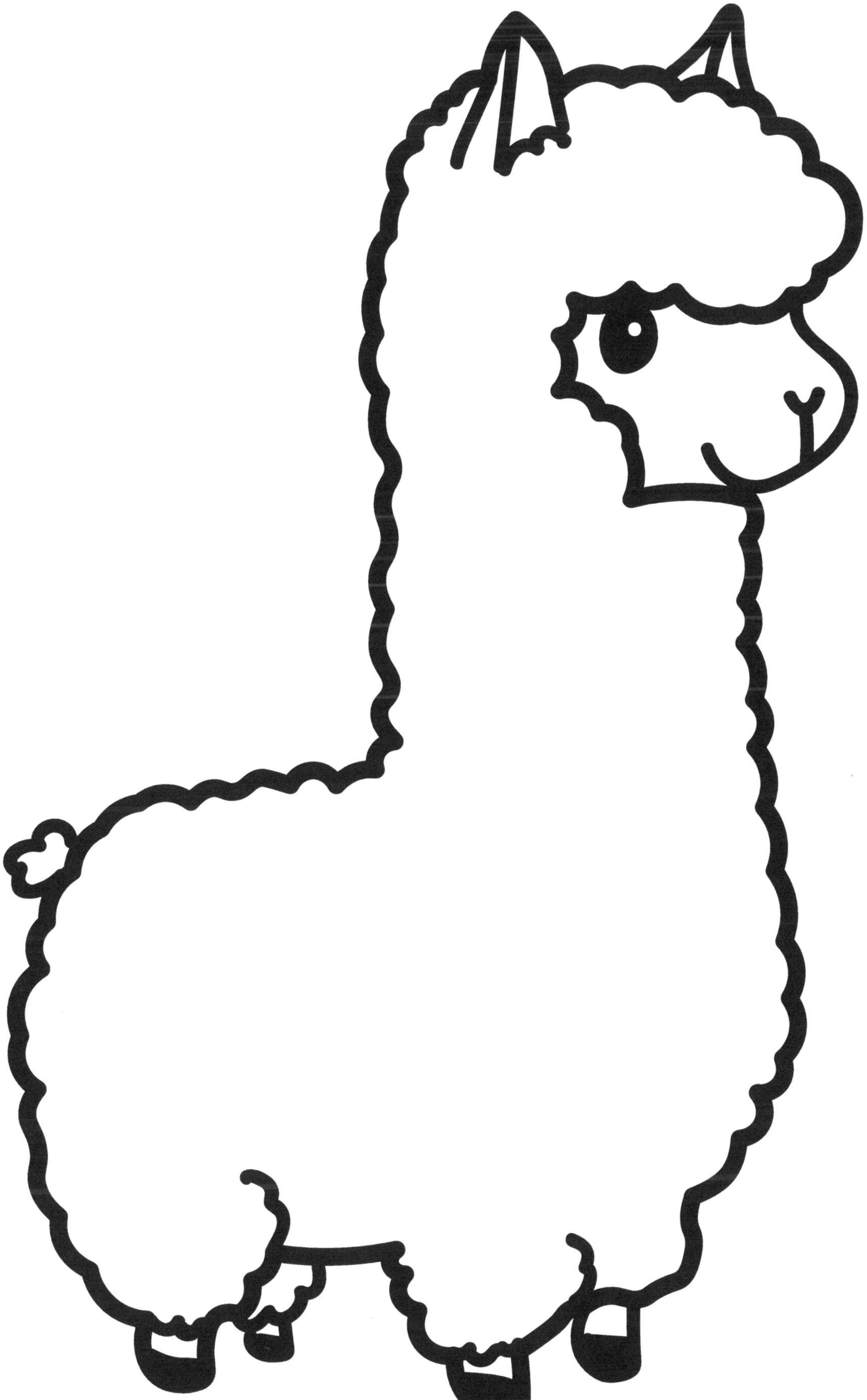

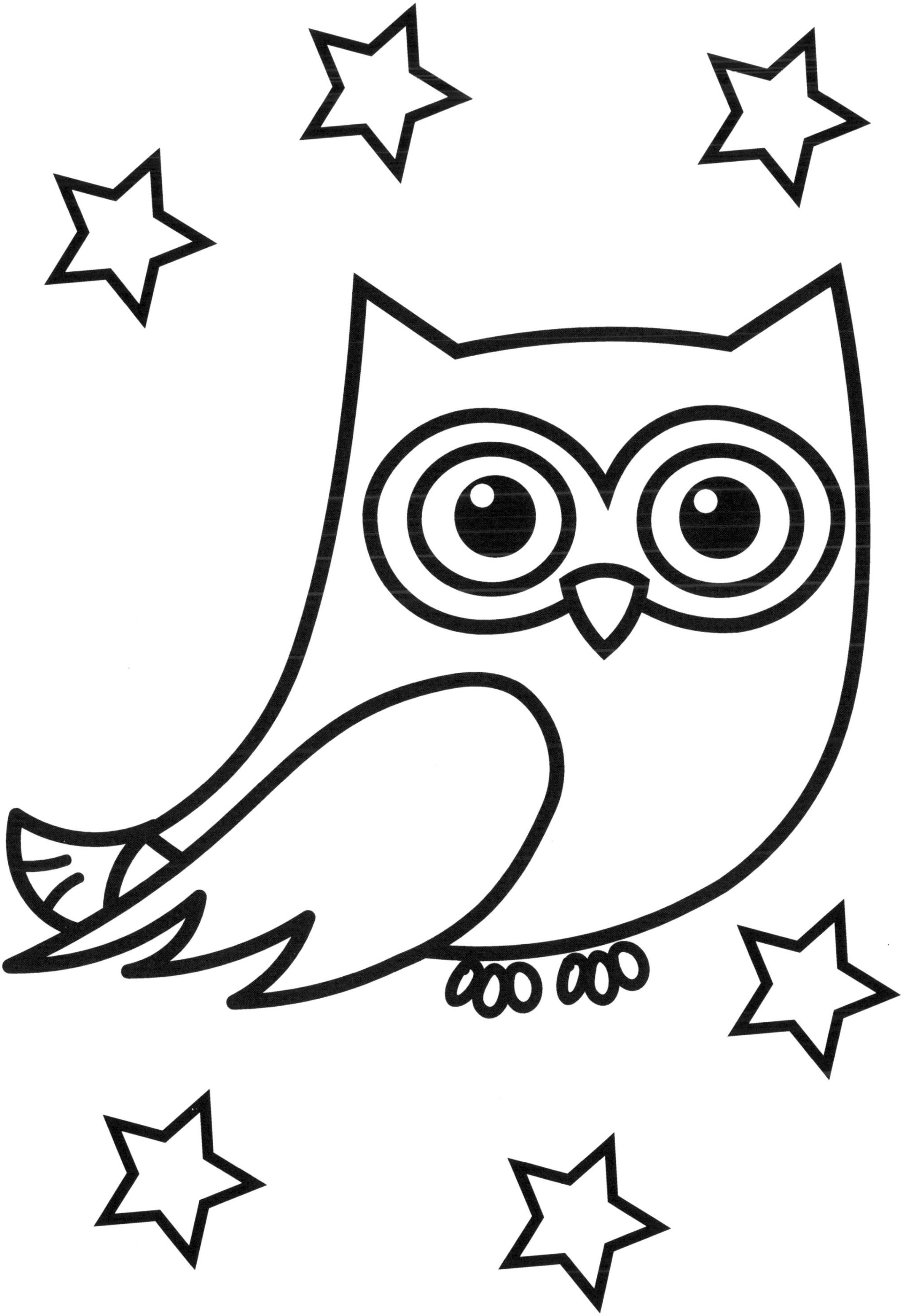

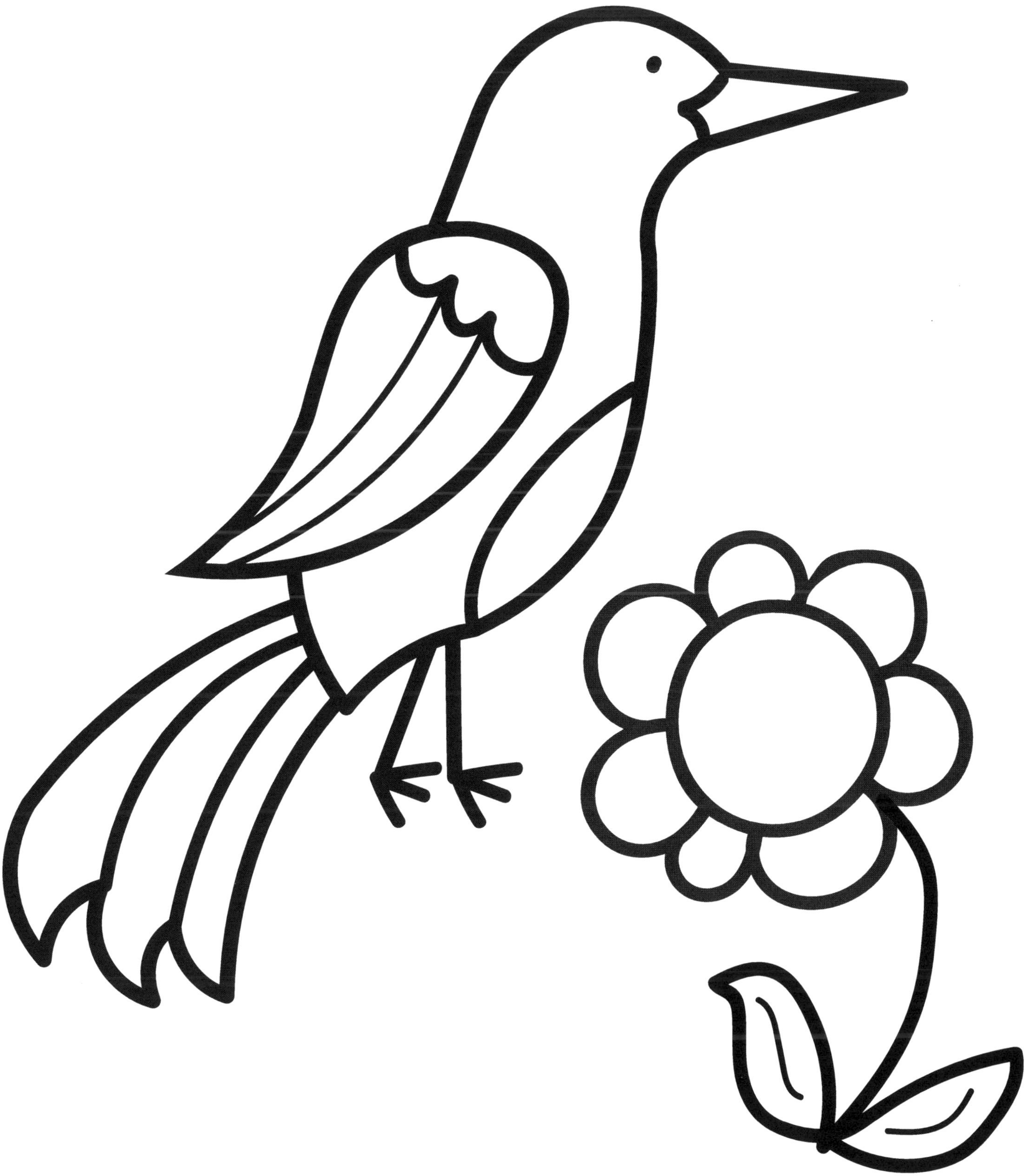

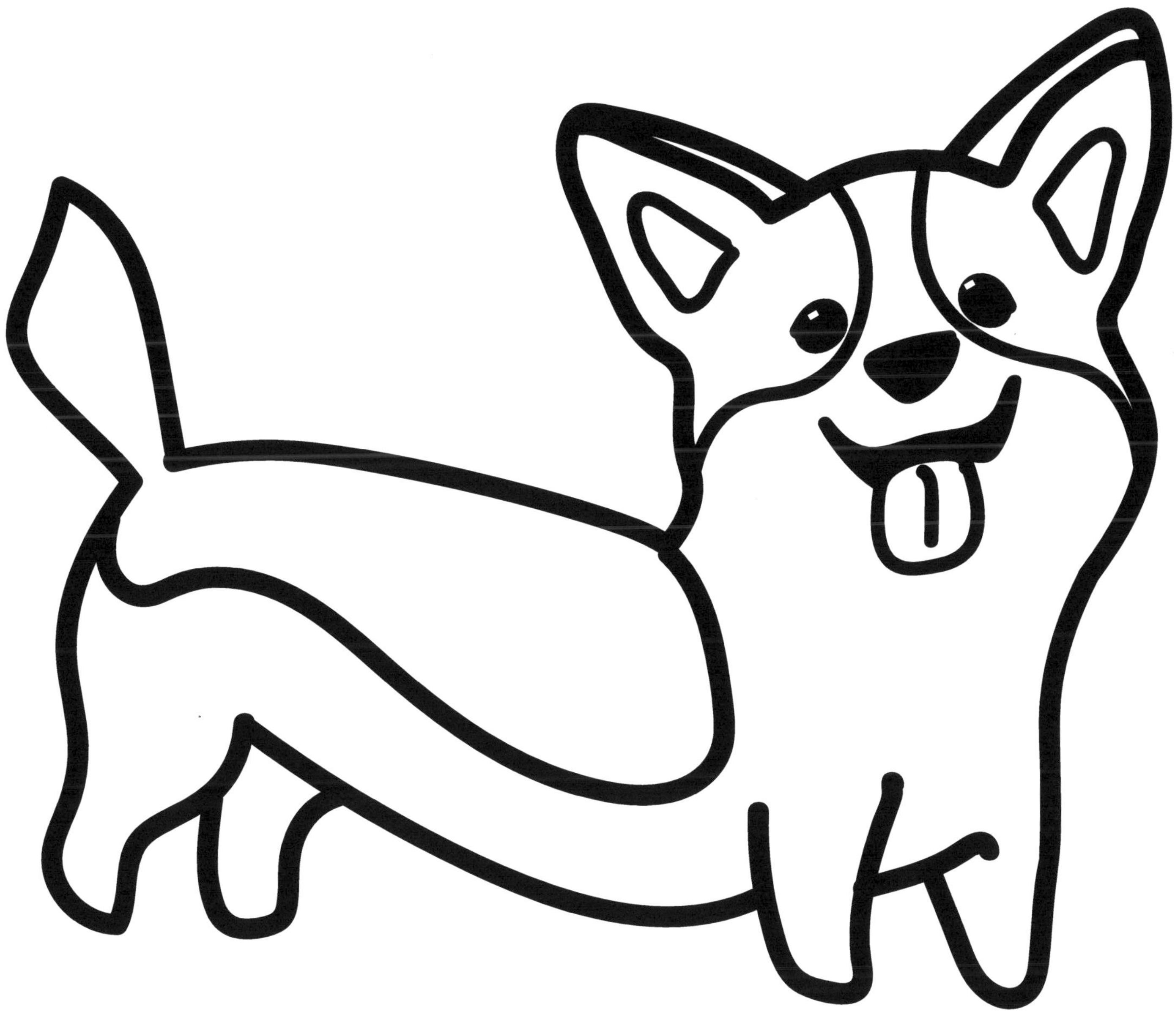

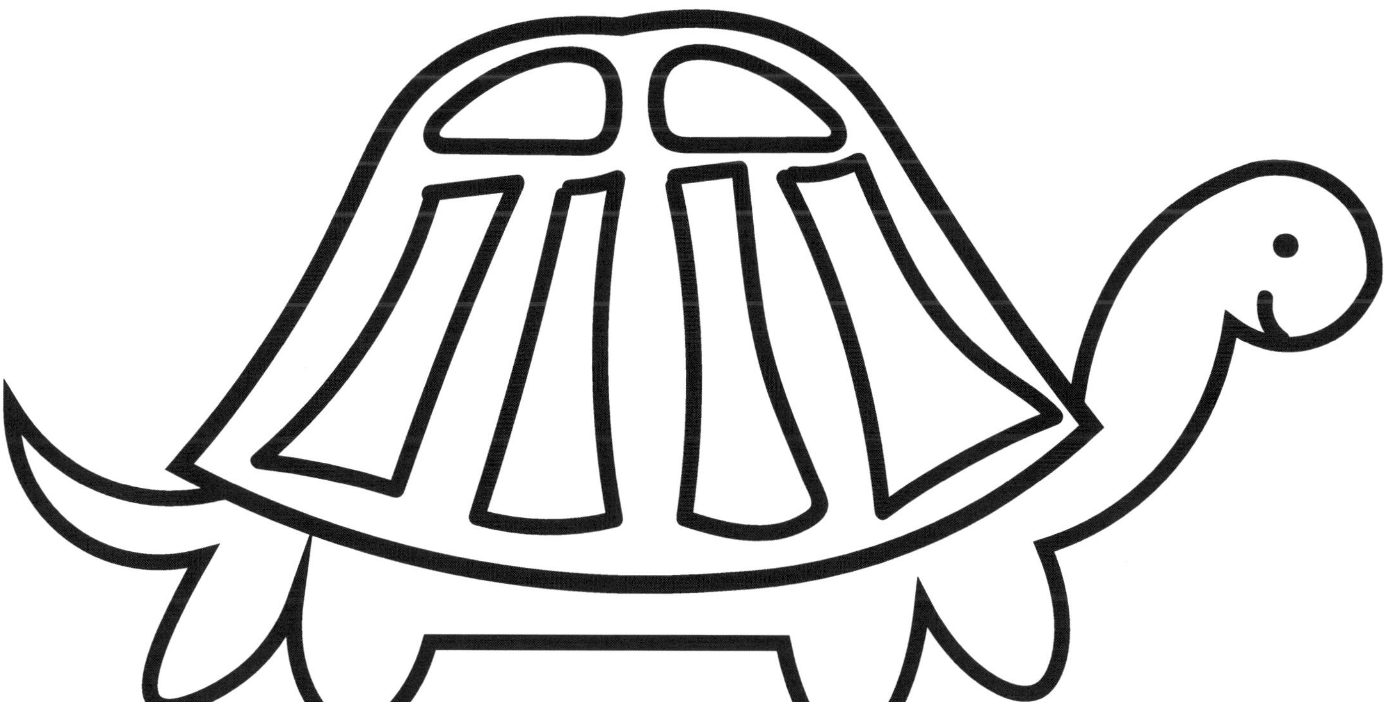

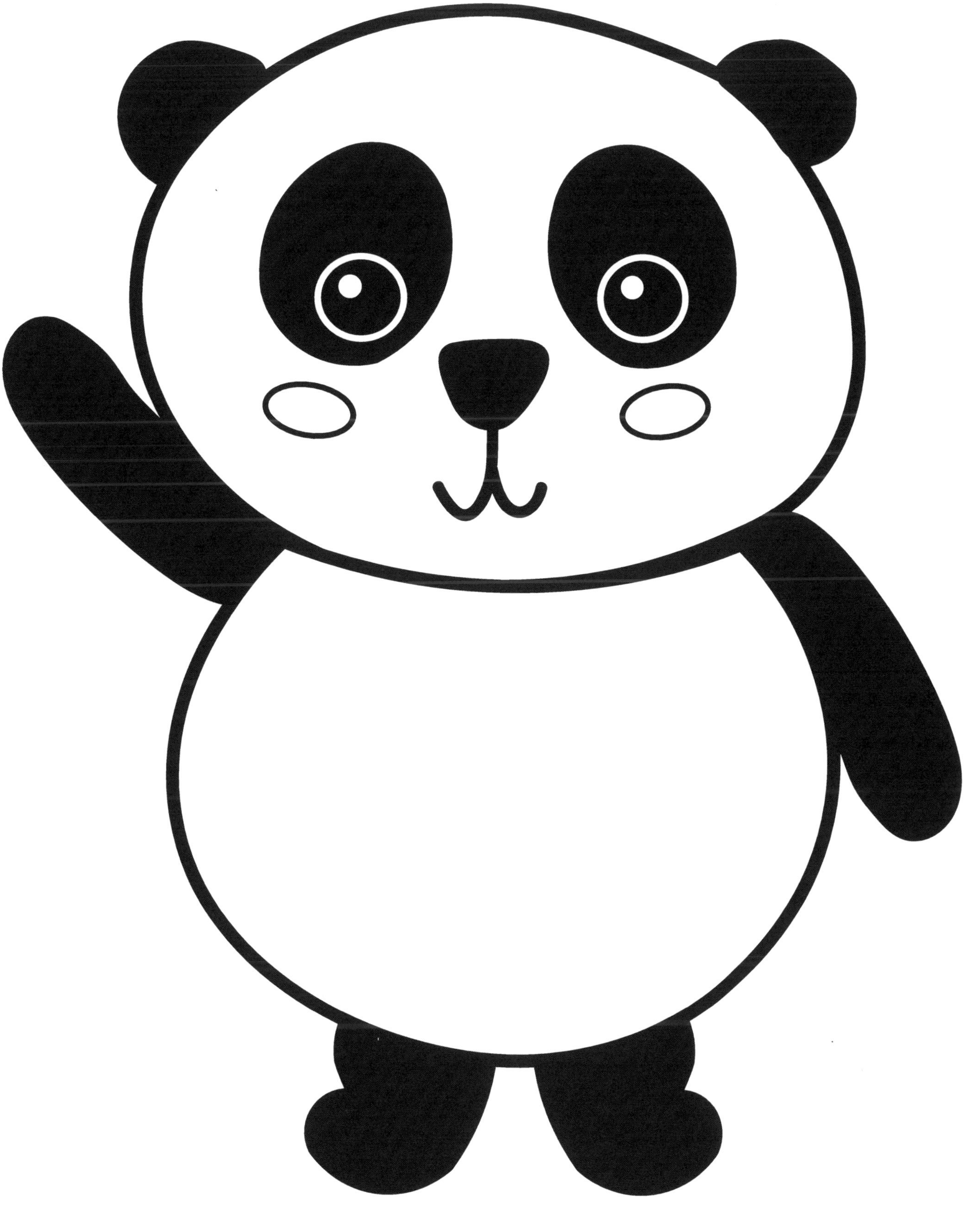

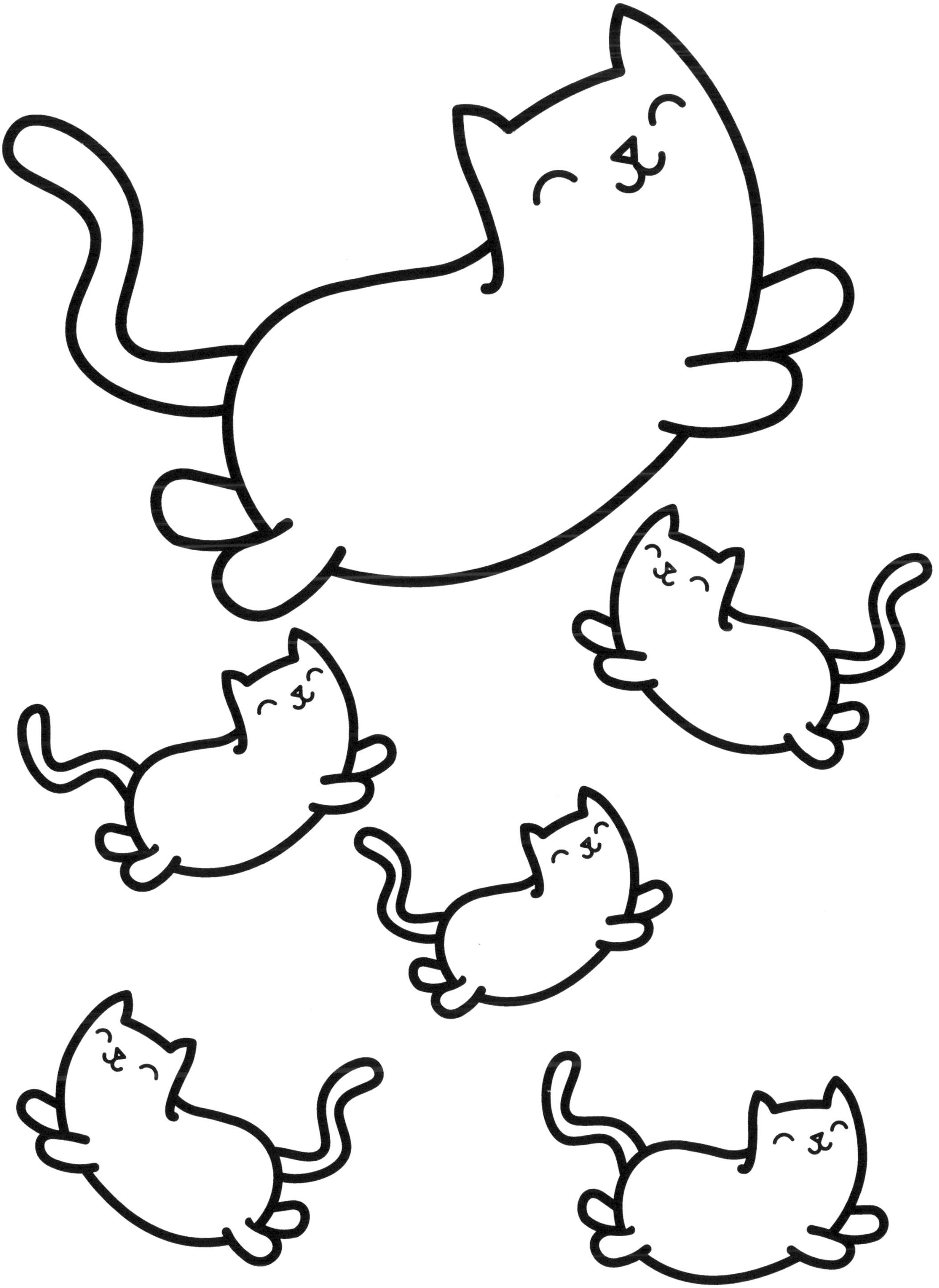

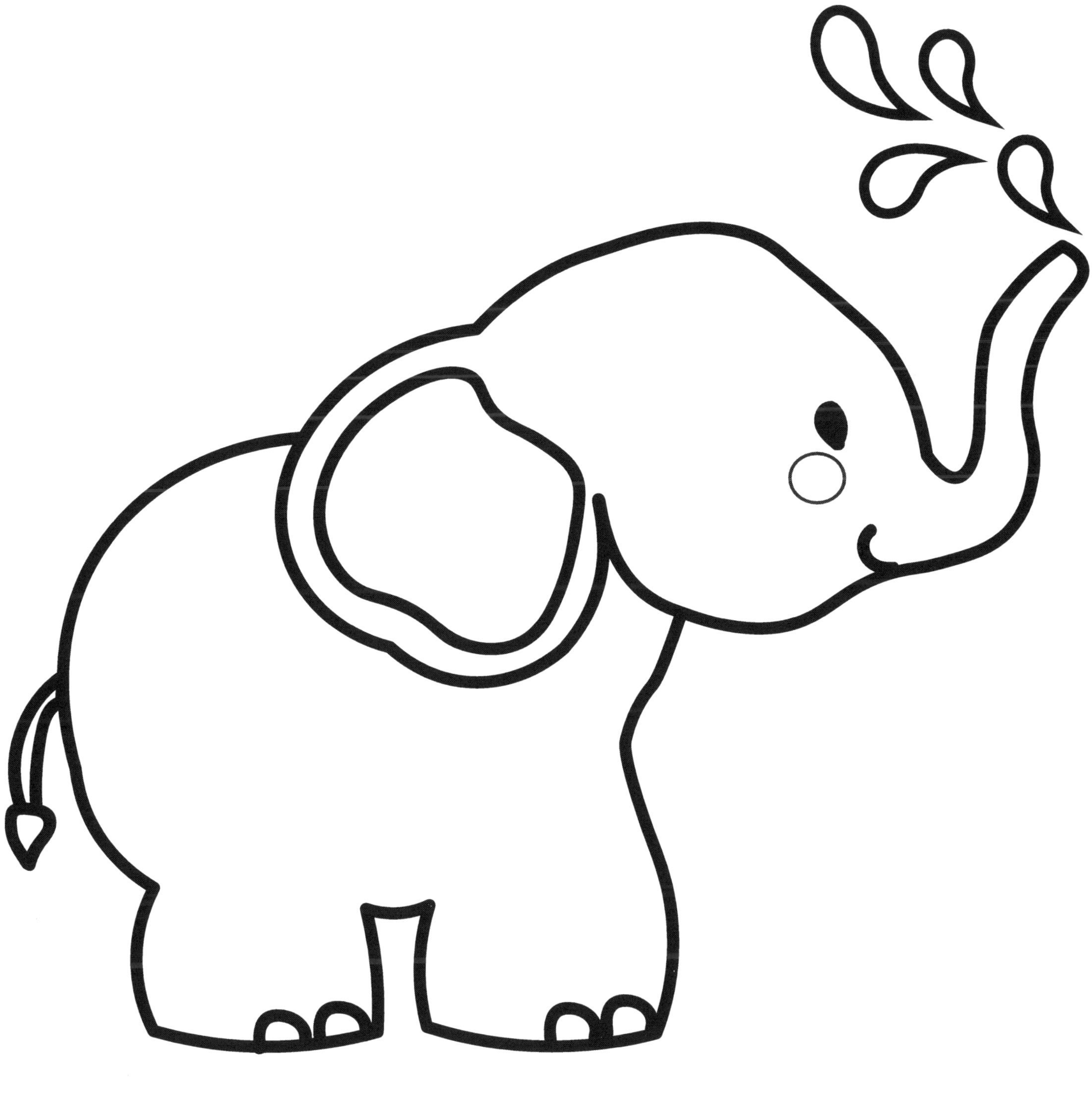

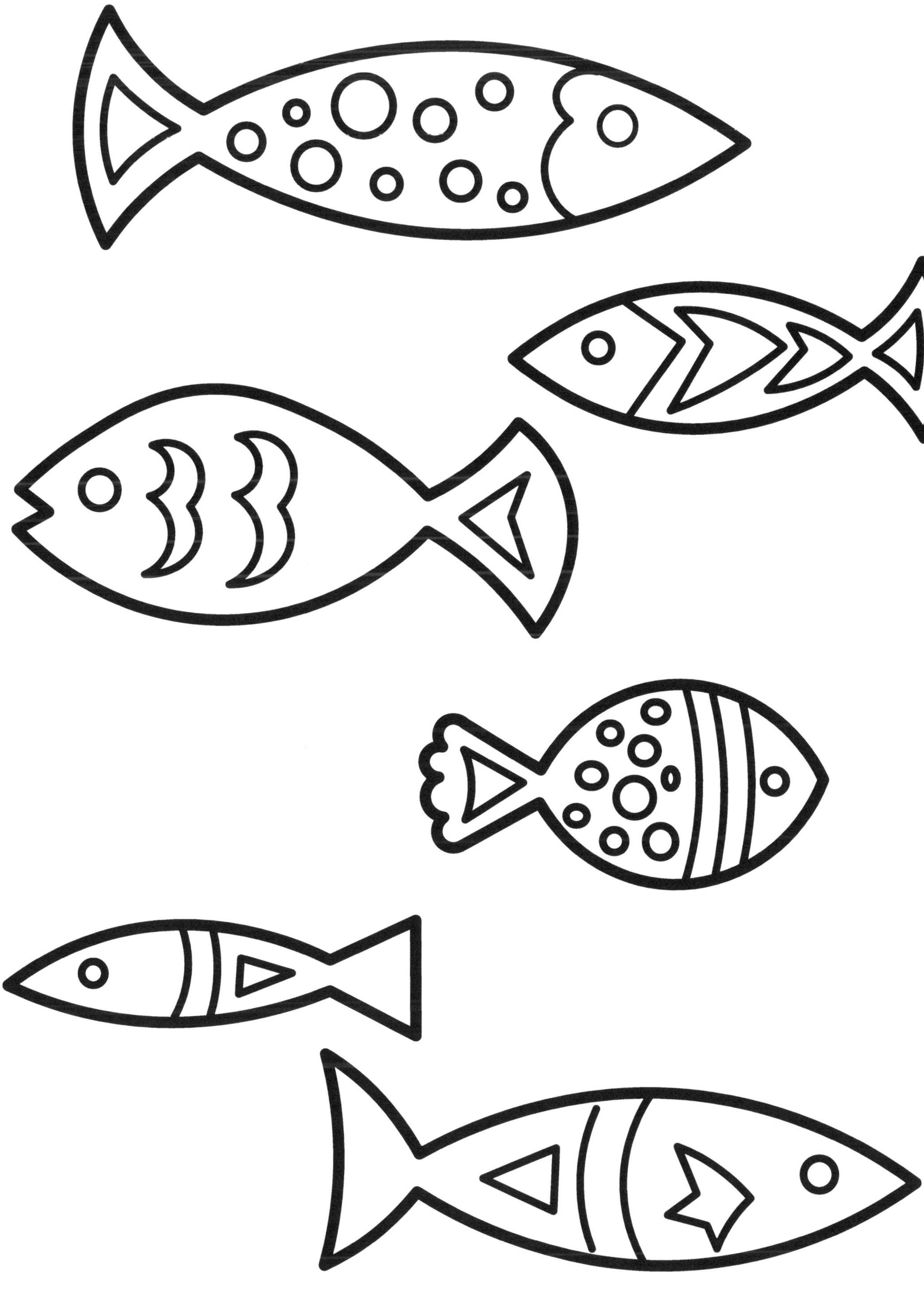

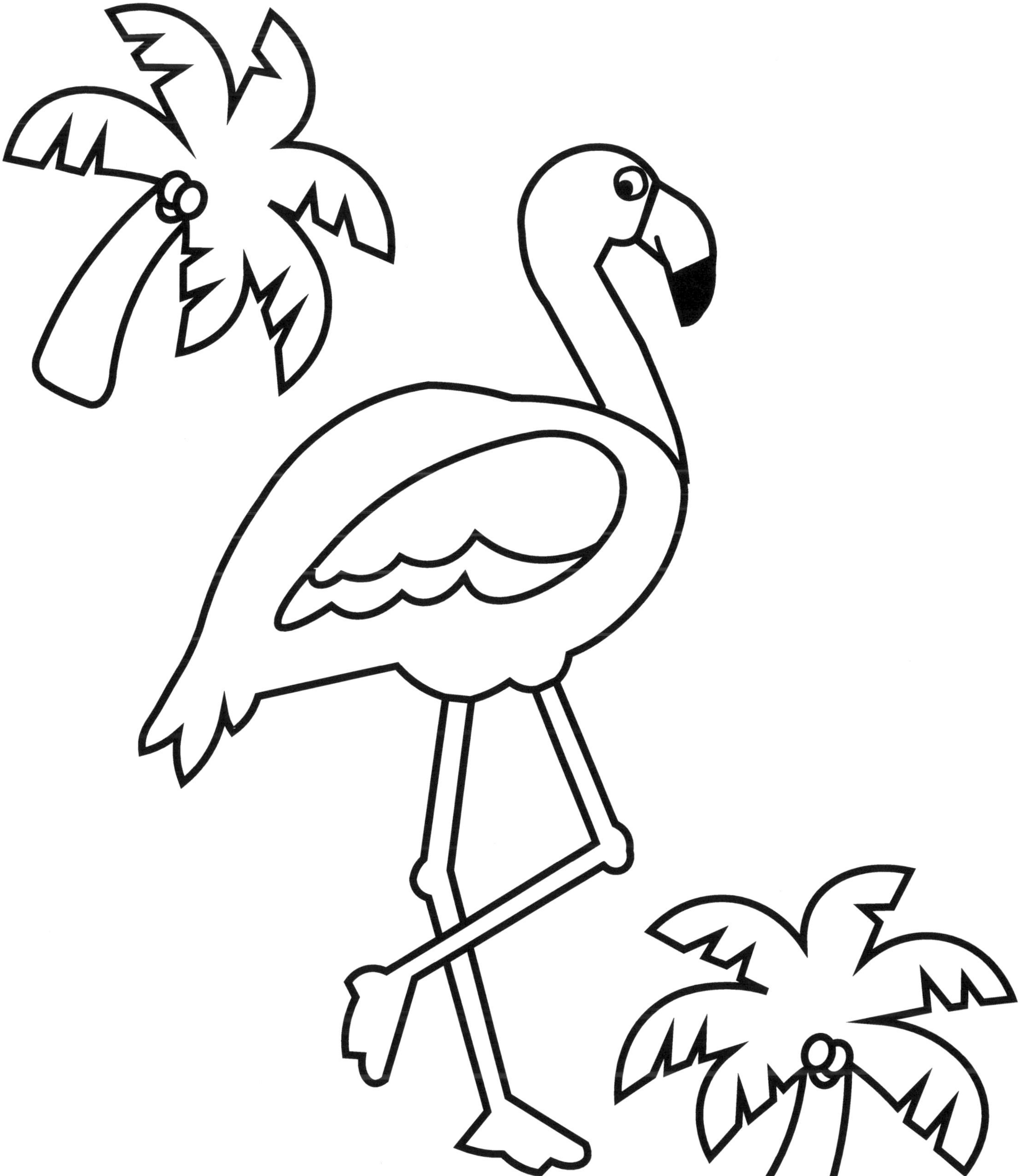

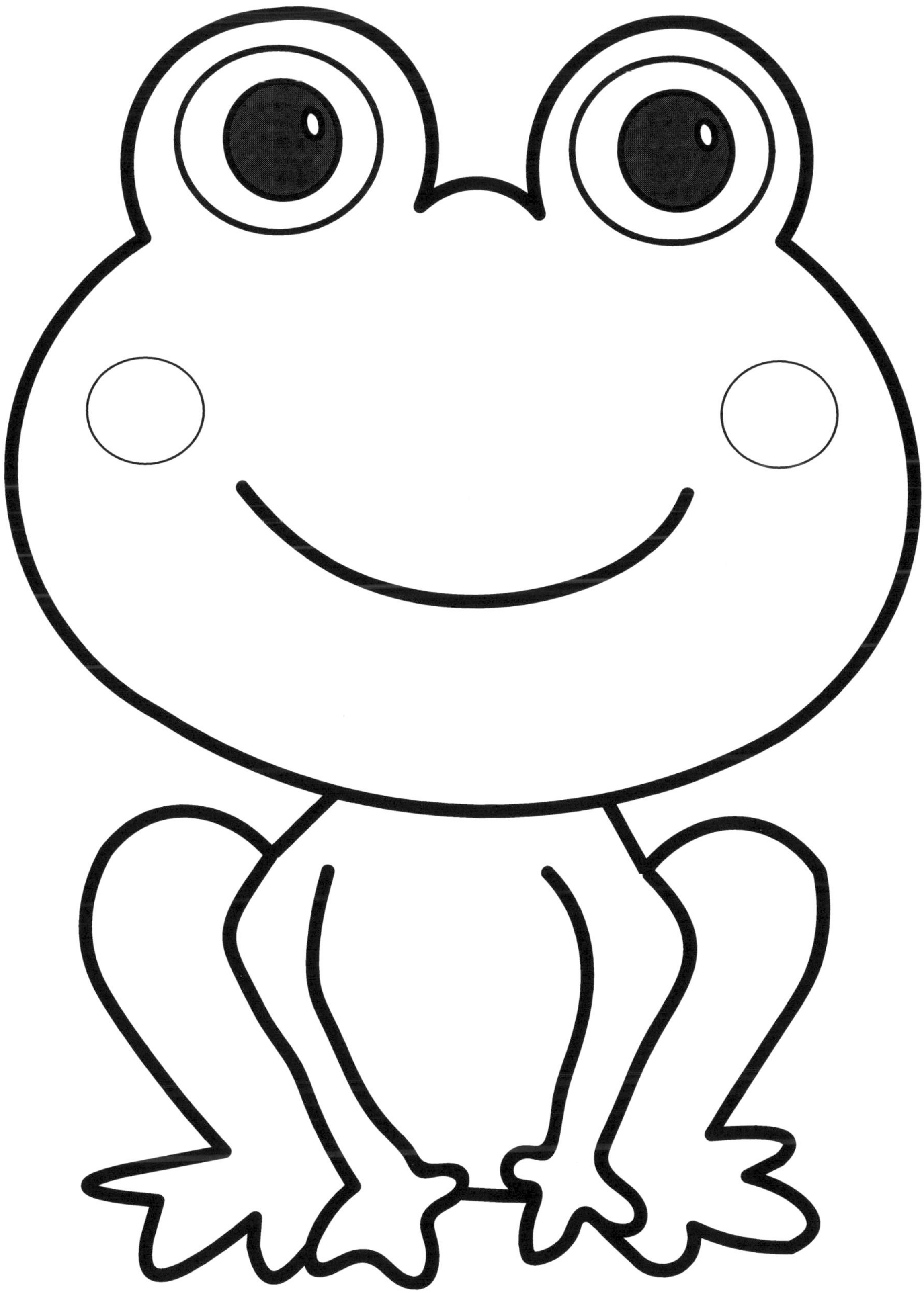

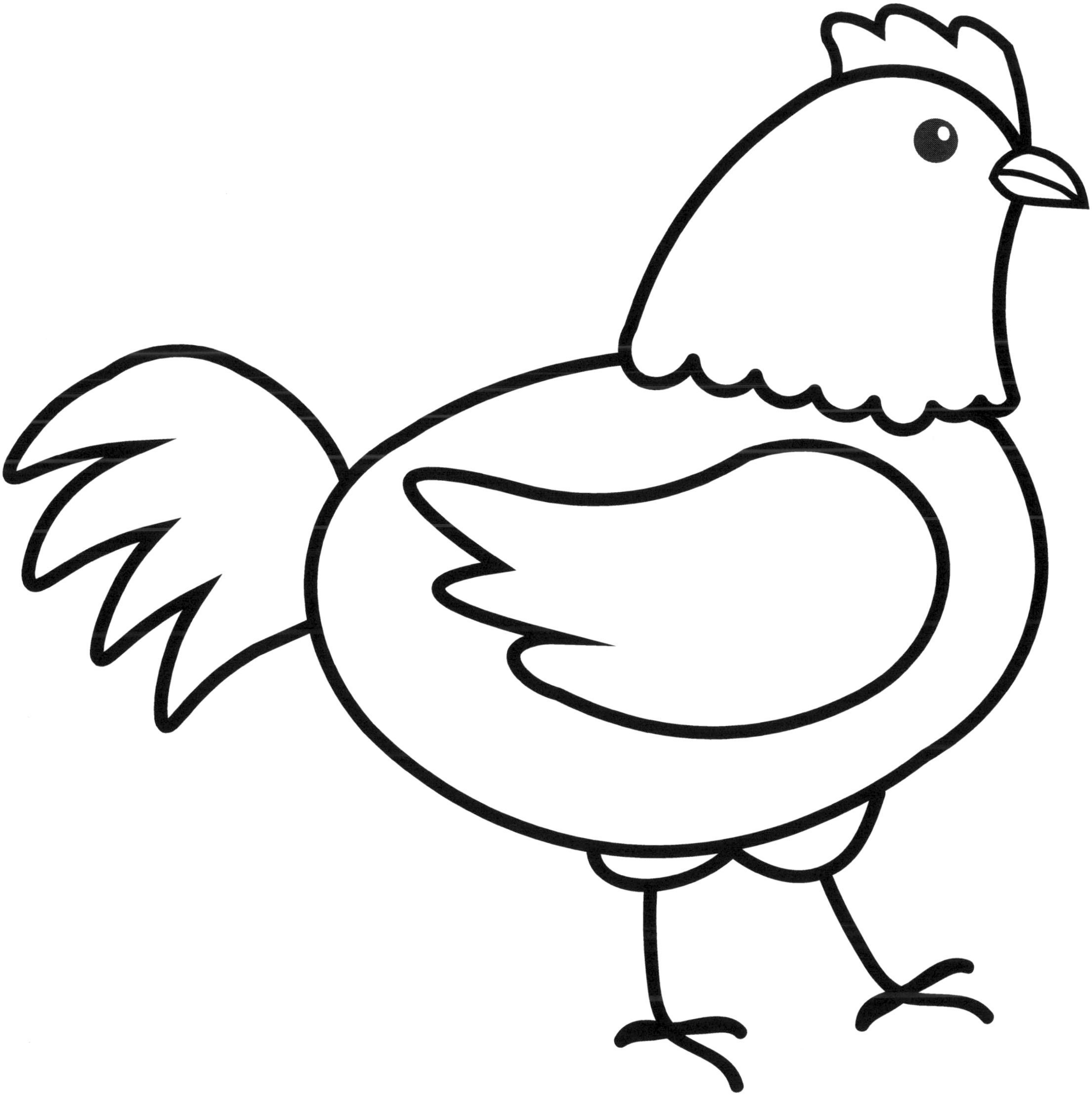

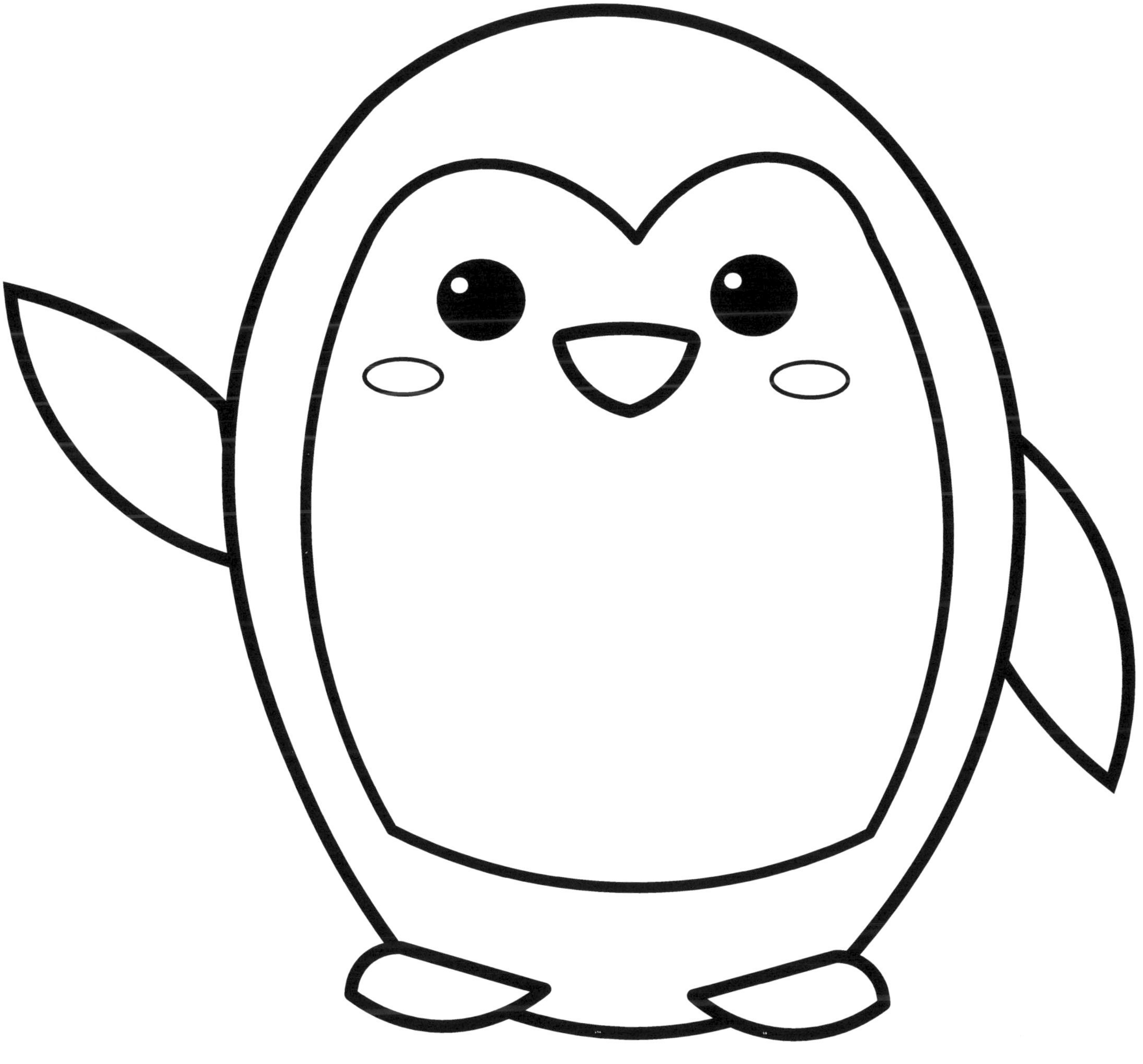

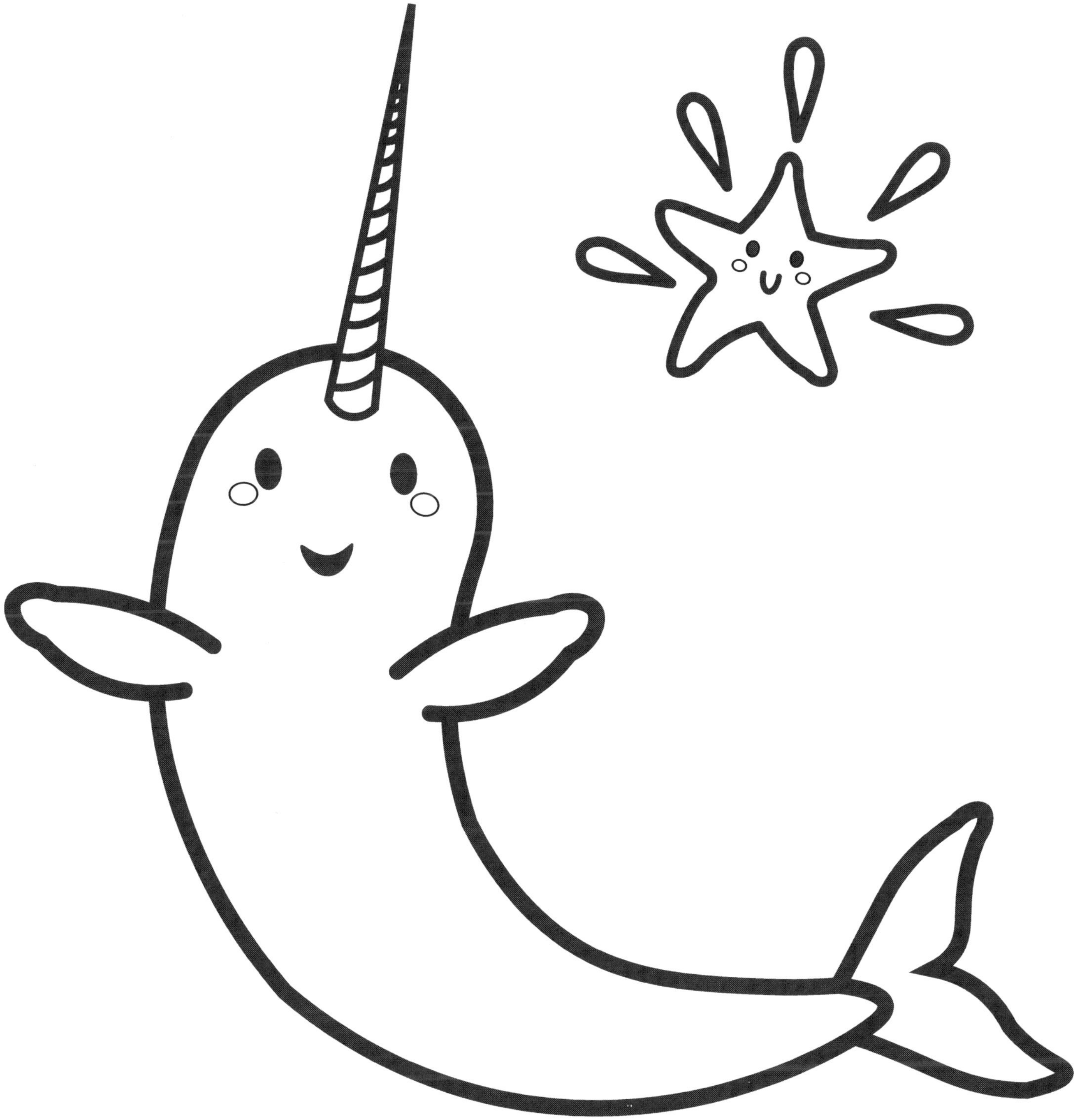

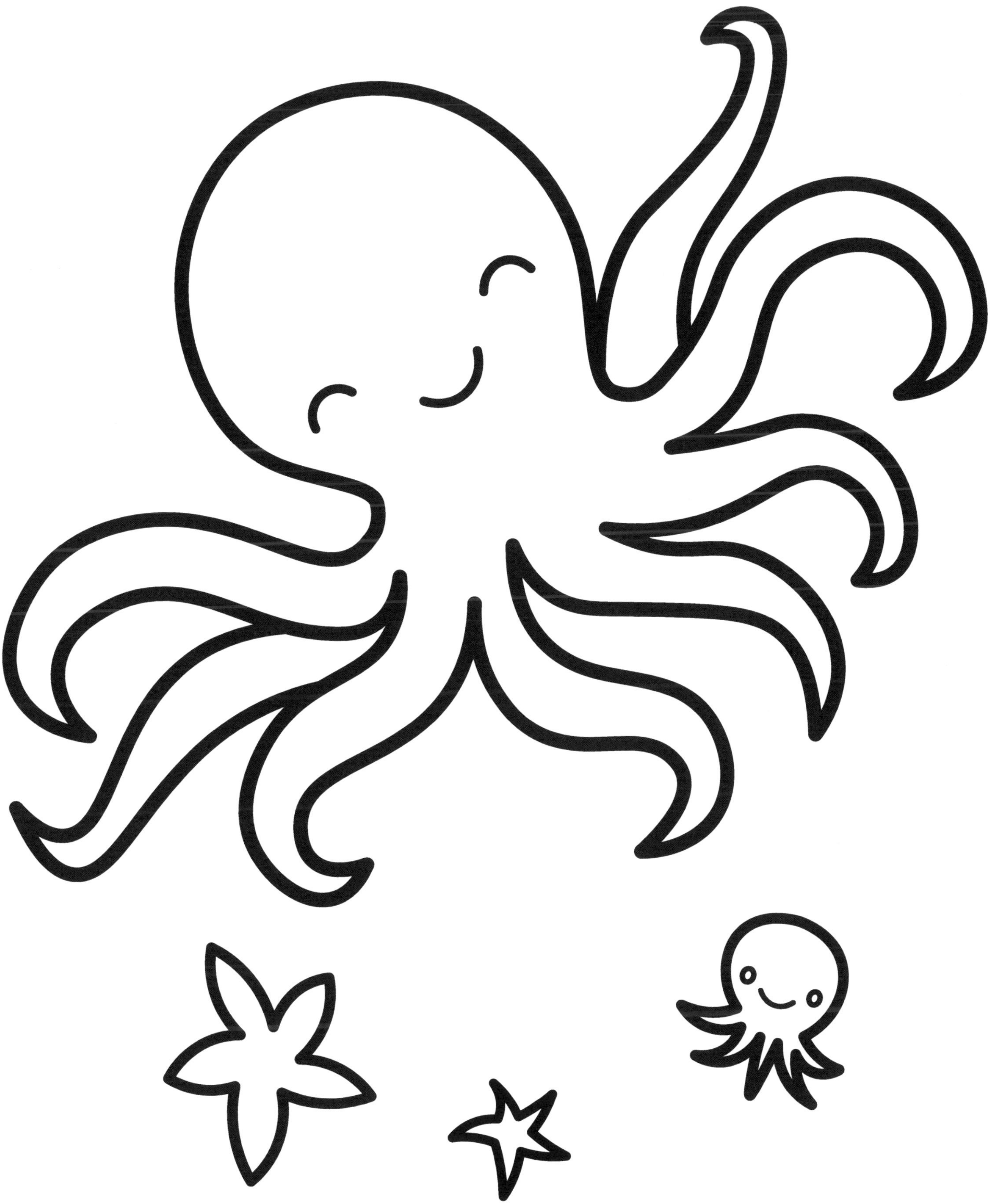

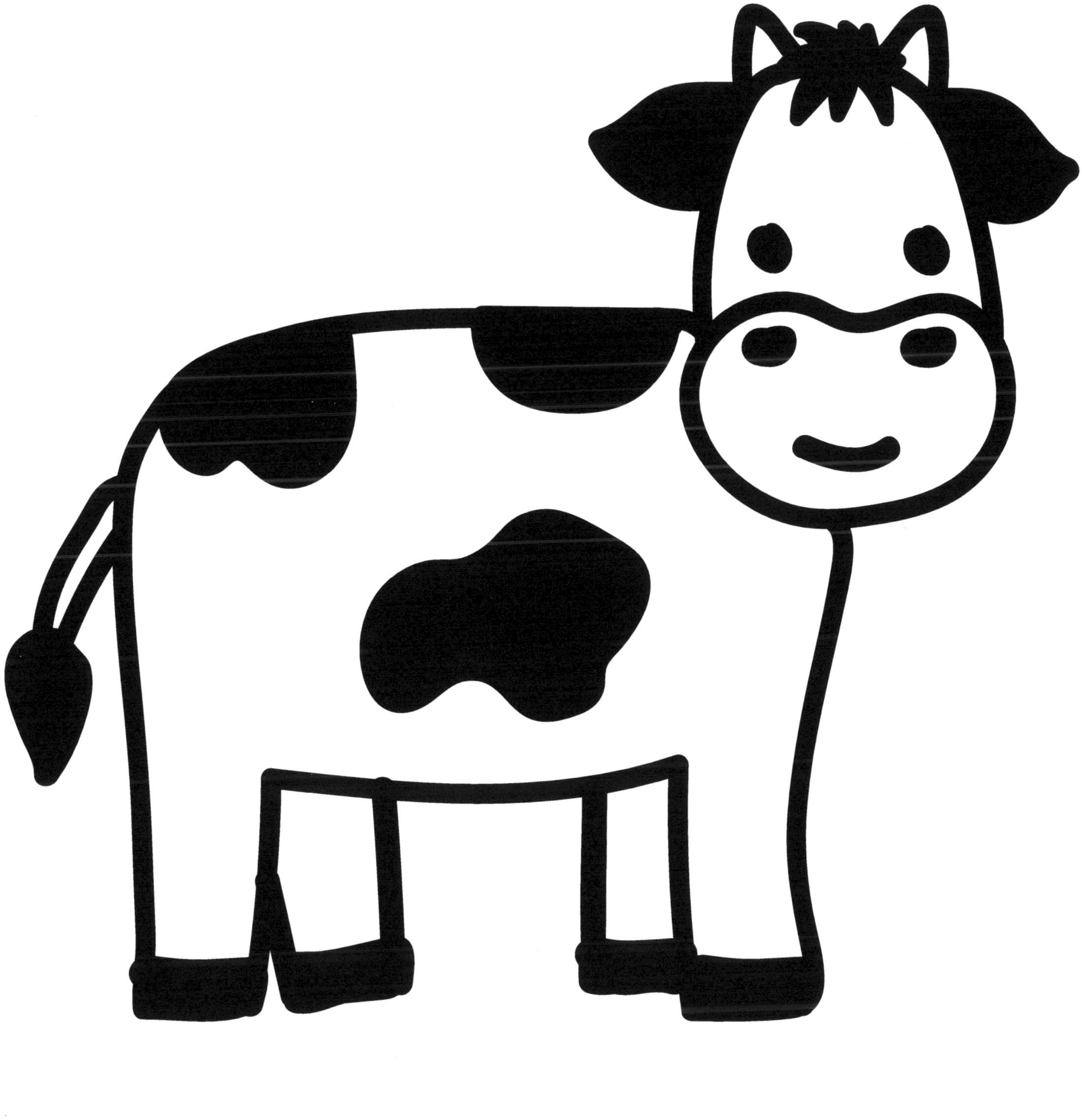

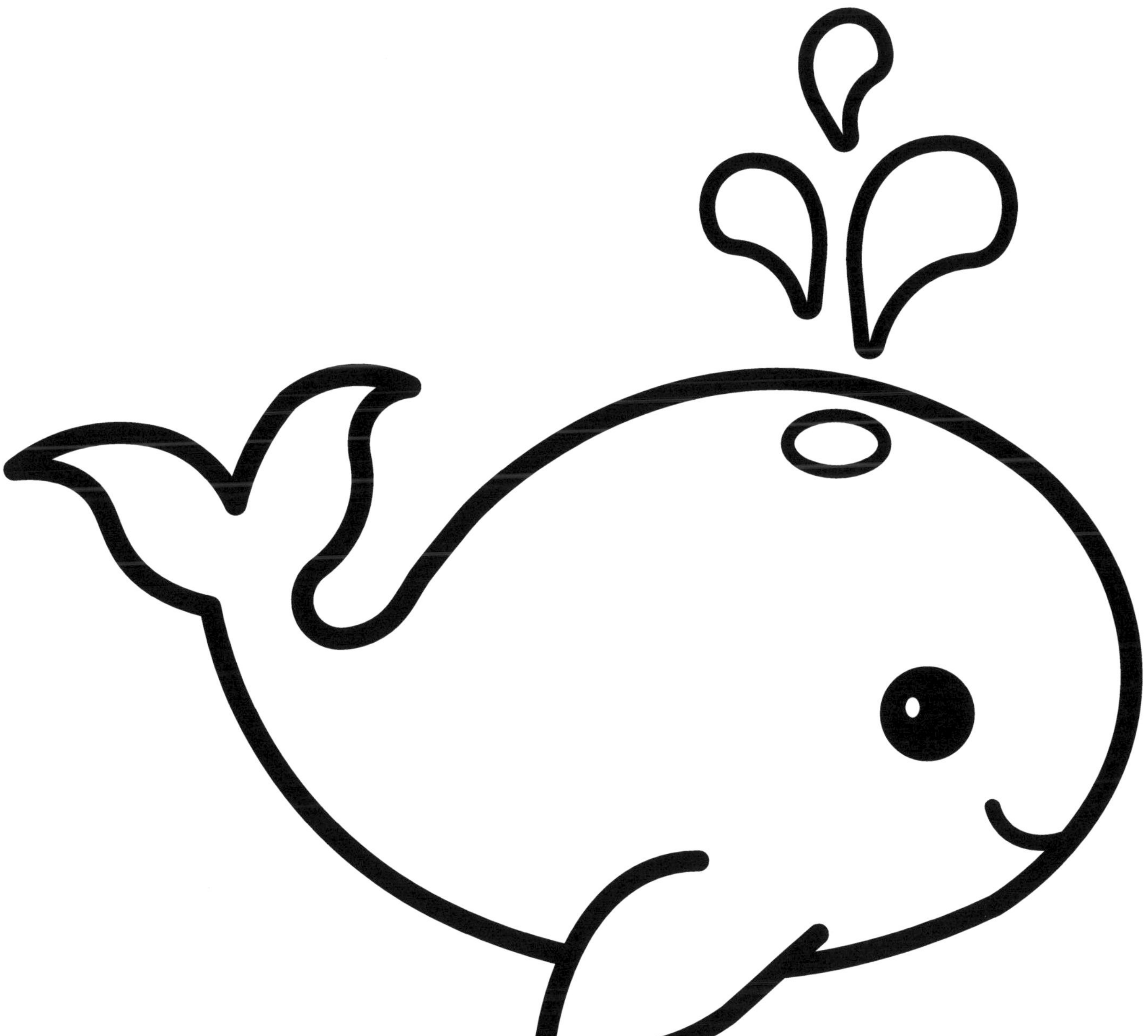

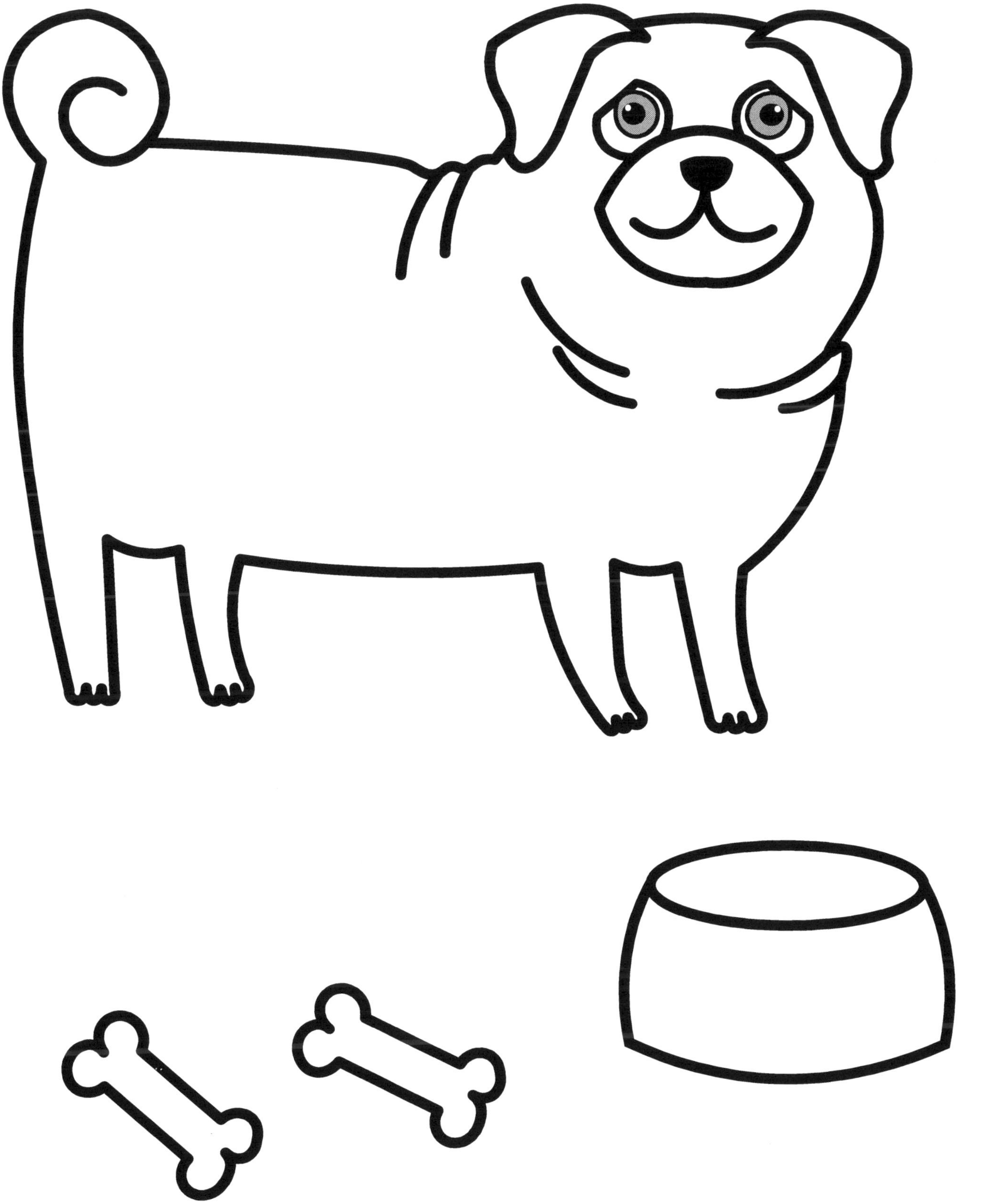

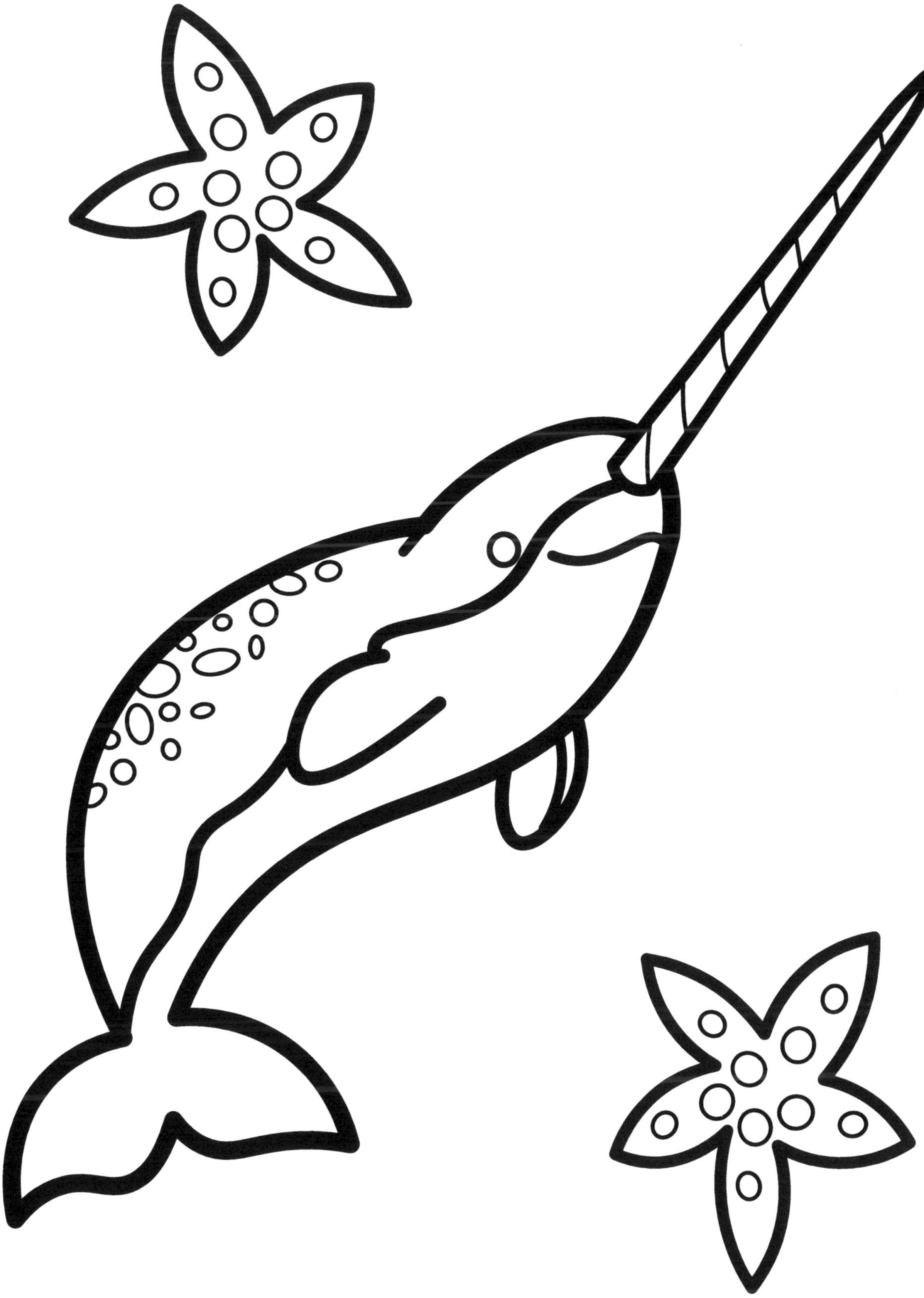

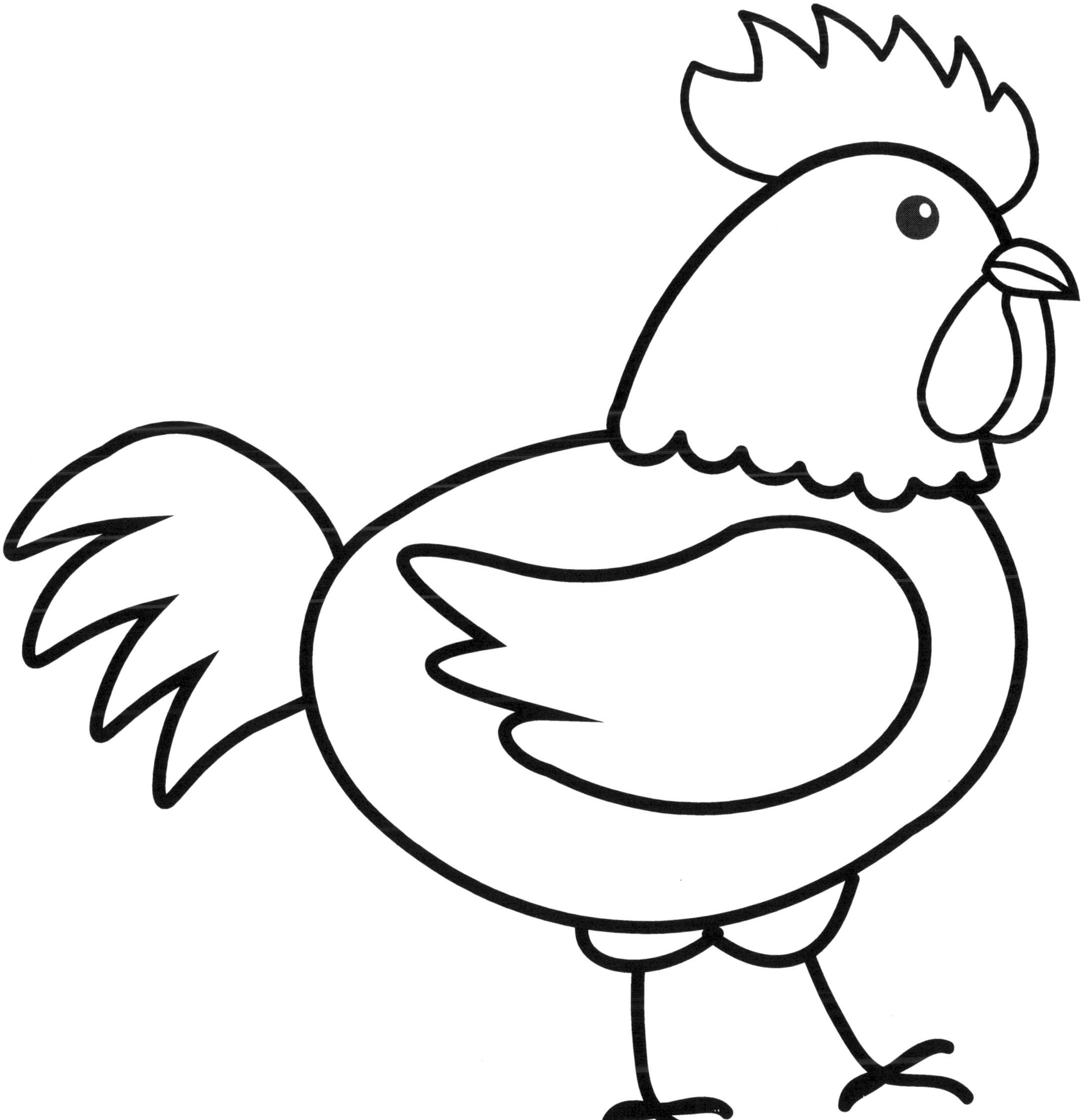

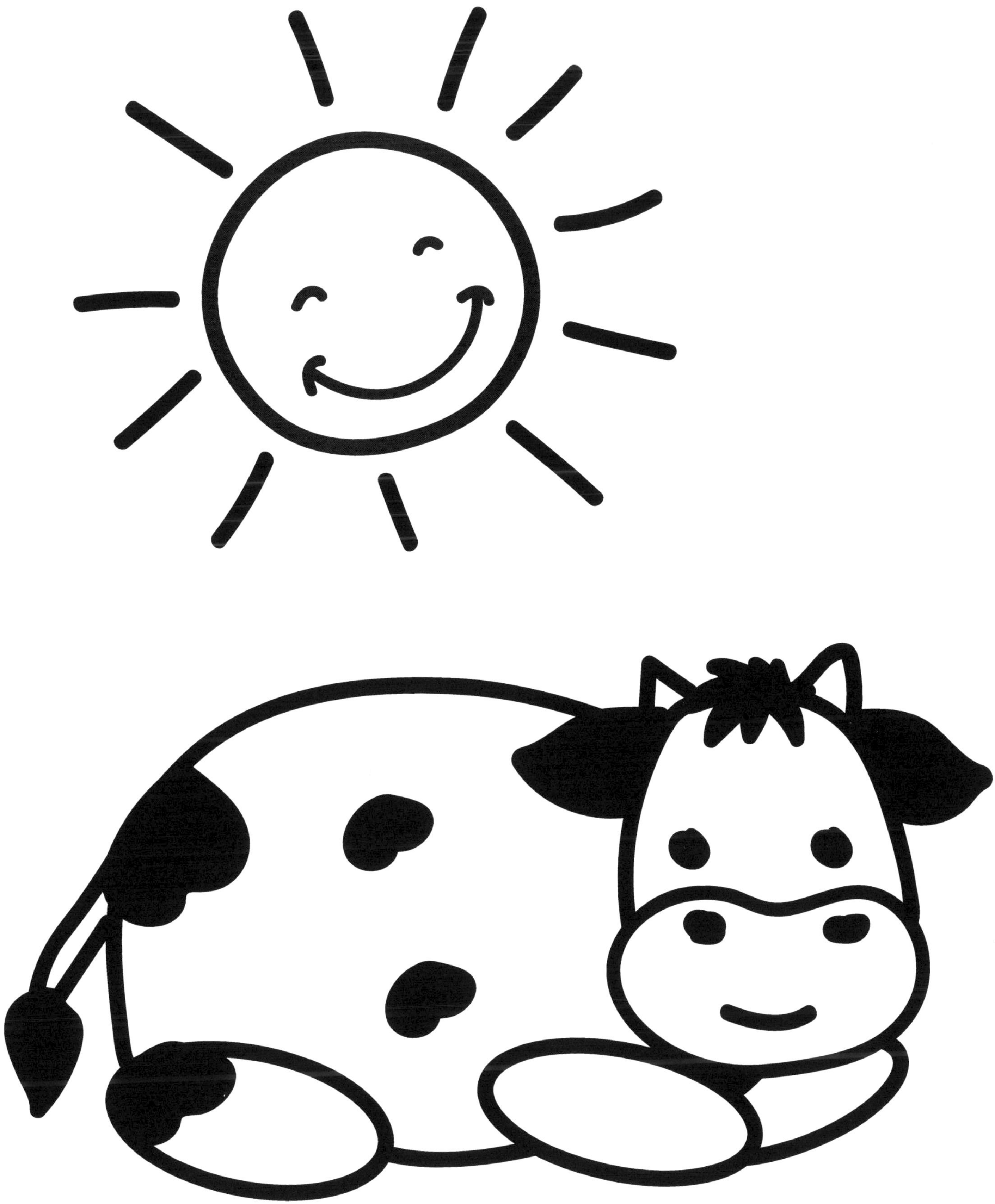

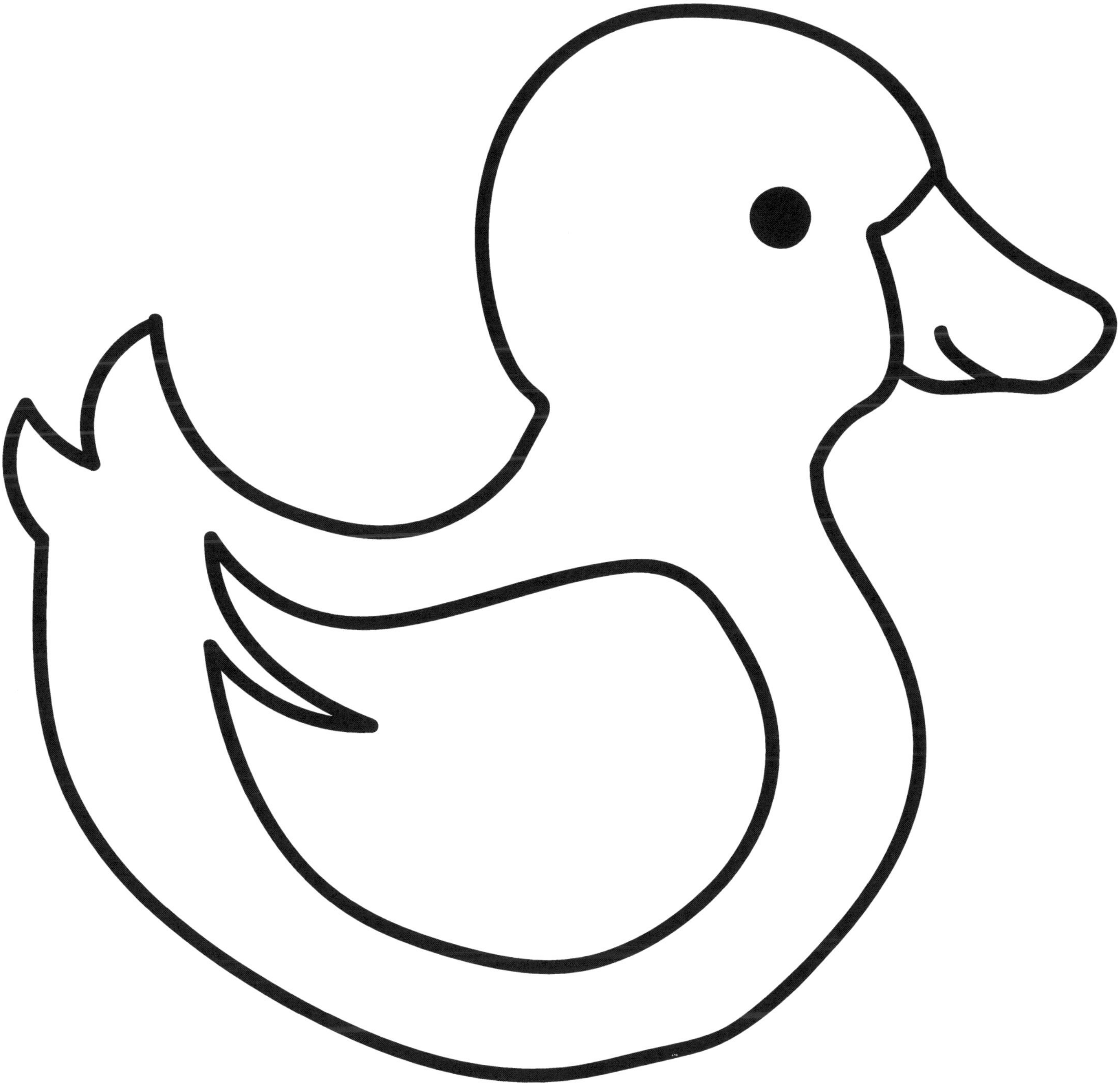

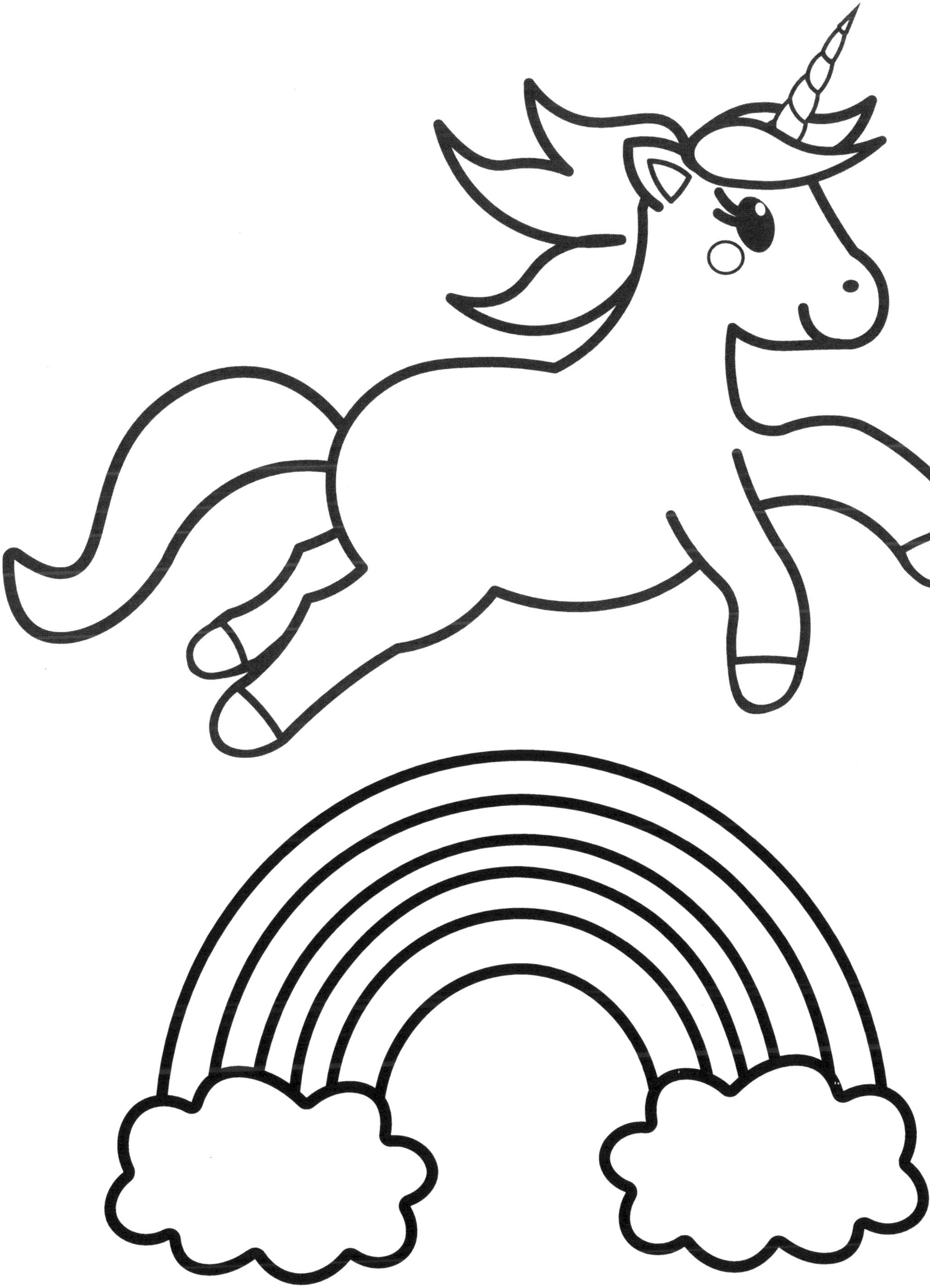

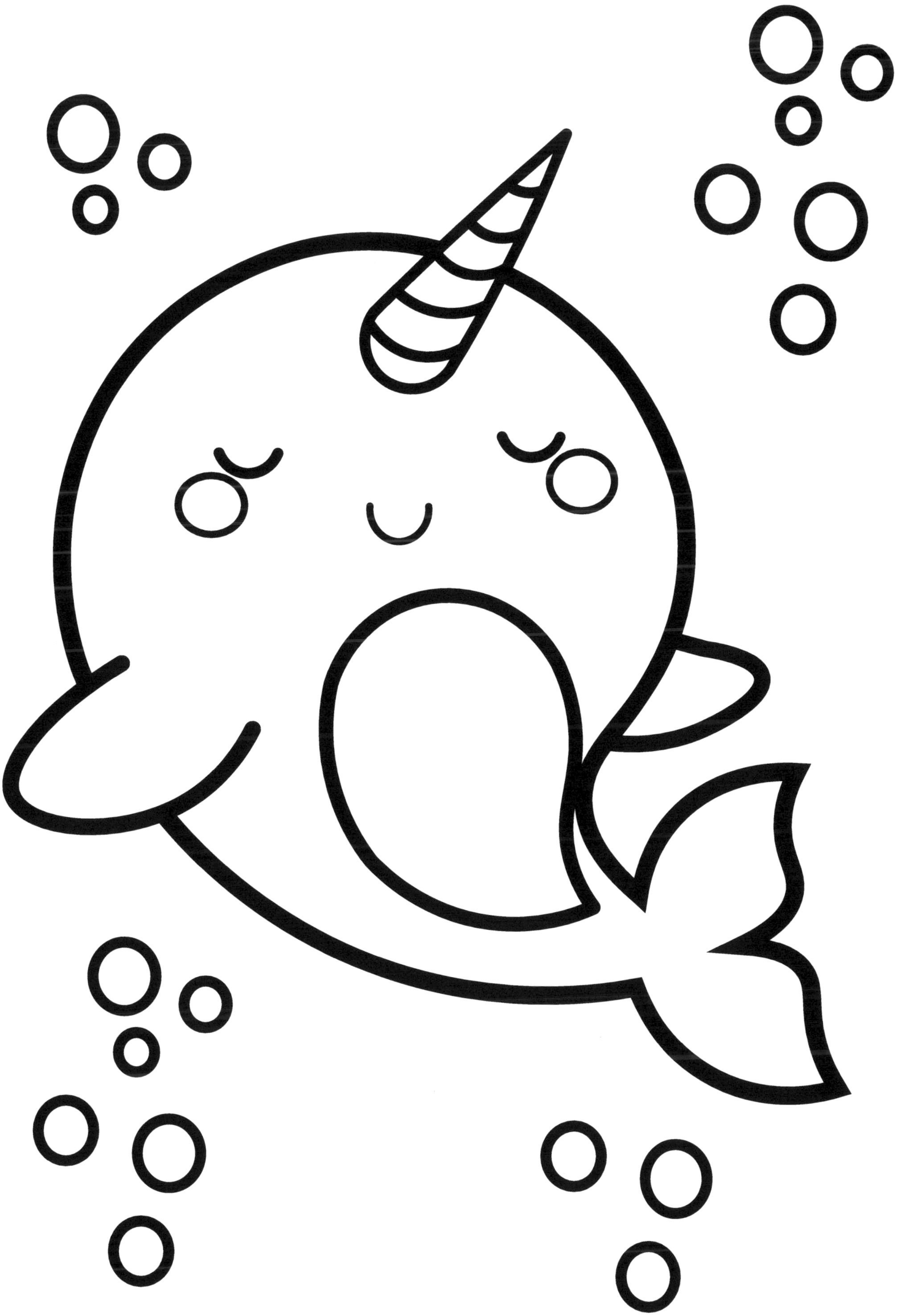

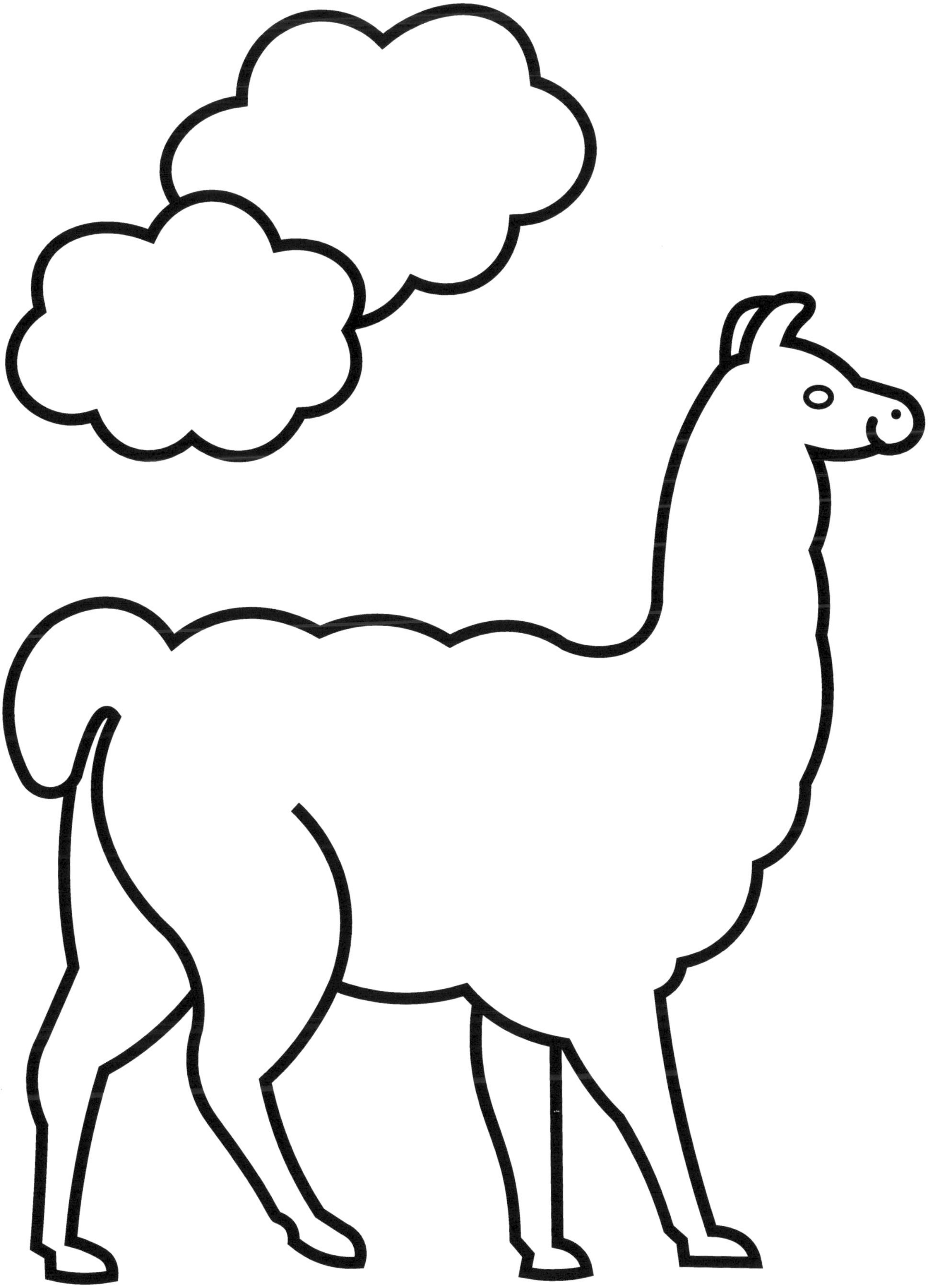

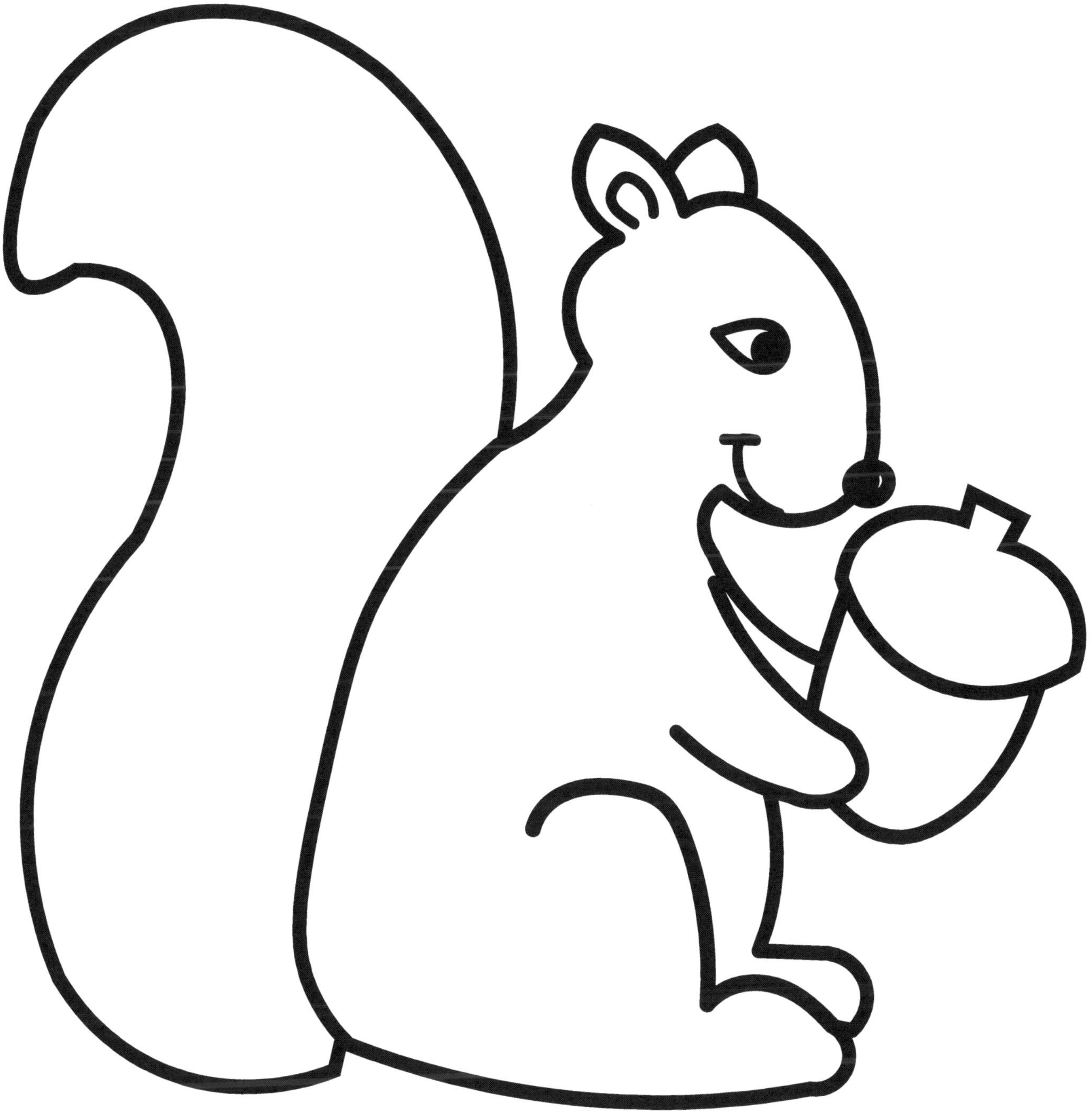

39109068R00060

Made in the USA
Middletown, DE
14 March 2019